Xtreme PREPAREDNESS!

BE PREPARED NOT SCARED

MR Valentine

XtremePreparedness.com

Copyright 2017

All Rights Reserved

Table of Contents

Introduction 4
Chapter 1 Situational Awareness 16
Chapter 2 Urban Situational Awareness 37
Chapter 3 Preparedness & Survival Mindset 50
Chapter 4 Preparedness 59
Chapter 5 Canning 73
Chapter 6 Off-The-Grid 87
Chapter 7 Tent Living 90
Chapter 8 Two-Wheel Bugging-Out! 95
Chapter 9 Safe Area & Eco-Villages 98
BONUS! 112

INTRODUCTION

It is my honor to have the opportunity to meet you through this short but hopefully insightful and instructive manual on Situational Awareness, Preparedness & Survival. This will be the sixth book I have written on the Preparedness and Survival niche. I see you, your loved ones, friends and colleagues benefiting from this very important training as it takes on more importance in these very troubling times of both potential man-made scenarios like terrorism and natural ones occurring at an increasingly alarming rate!

I wrote my first book *A Family Survival Manual for Y2K & Beyond* at the time we thought that the world as we knew it could be disastrously disrupted by not being prepared for a glitch in coding of ones and zeros that became the code name "Y2K". We went on Code Red and had coding experts in Cobalt going 24-7 trying to correct the glitch so that planes did not fall out if the sky; banks would continue to dispense money; stores would stay open; weapons of mass destruction protecting our country would still function; etc.

Due to the valiant efforts of these decoders working frantically right up to the dawn of the year 2000 we avoided this catastrophe so we could celebrate the New Millennium! I was not going to take any chances that the efforts would fail so I prepared myself along with several friends, if the code had not been repaired. I came to a beautiful retreat called Rose Creek with these friends from Atlanta. As soon as the all clear was sounded on Y2K many of my friends returned to Atlanta; however several of us decided to stay. I have lived in the Franklin, North Carolina area now for over 17 years.

I like so many other people went back to being "asleep" not expecting anything that could disrupt us until there was what has become "911" destroying the New York City World Trade Center and taking the lives of over 3000; a section of the Pentagon hit by jet in Washington, DC causing more deaths, and finally another jet liner plummeting to a Pennsylvania field leading to the deaths of all aboard. Then President Bush promised retribution and we are still fighting the War on Terrorism against mostly Islamic nations like my ancestors the Knights Templar did in the Holy Crusades.

It is for what has continued to happen regarding terrorism; three devastating killer hurricanes in a 30 day period and most recently the shootings in Texas and California that I continue to research and write books on Situational Awareness, Preparedness and Survival like this one directed at you.

This one focuses on SITUATIONAL AWARENESS and is by far one of the most important books I have written. Today we see too many of us NOT SITUATIONALLY AWARE! We are too wrapped up in one of the BIGGEST enemies of SITUATIONAL AWARENESS – the smartphone! To terrorists these smartphones can be one of the BEST things to come along! I see far too many people today, who have NO clue as to what is happening around them as they bury their heads and attention into the screen of a smartphone!

Don't get me wrong. There have been numerous incidents when people who were AWARE saved lives of people and alerted the authorities as to trouble they were witnessing. I am enthralled with the new CBS TV show *Wisdom of the Crowd*! For those of you not familiar with the show it uses people who have downloaded an app called "Sophie" named after the creator's daughter, who was murdered. The original intention of the app was to find her murderer; however it also becomes useful for stopping serial killers and other murderers.

Actually I have made contact with the REAL Walter O'Brien's team about creating a SITUATIONAL AWARENESS app like "Sophie". Many of you have watched like myself the CBS TV show *Scorpion* maybe not realizing there is a REAL Walter O'Brien, who has worked with the military and does have a IQ north of 200! It would be his team that could make my SITUATIONAL AWARENESS app a reality!

Until then, I want to teach you what I have learned about this LIFESAVING training that is used by SWAT, US Special Forces, US Border Patrol, etc. I consider this the MOST important aspect of the Preparedness and Survival niche that I have been involved in for over 17 years.

As I mentioned before, most of us have only become aware of the so-called indispensable SMARTPHONE! We are FOCUSED on this tiny screen for text messages, what others are saying on Facebook, and other pastimes.

Terrorists and criminals don't want you AWARE of your surroundings or what is happening! This is what leads to carjacking while pumping gas. This is what leads to a thief making off with your mall purchases because you were too busy looking at that screen and not being AWARE! It could also lead to a suicide bomber exploding himself/herself in a US mall especially during the busy Holiday Season! I try to tell in my videos at at my SituationalAwareness.Expert (http://www.situationalawareness.expert) how you must be ALERT and AWARE more than ever before! It is not a matter of IF but only a matter of WHEN we experience a disastrous terroristic attack again on US soil!

You will be learning SITUATIONAL AWARENESS techniques developed by Tom Brown, my mentor and in my opinion the BEST teacher there is on Planet Earth! The US military agree as they regularly hire Tom to see if he can infiltrate top secret bases. He has NEVER failed in completing his mission! Why? He is the EXPERT on SITUATIONAL AWARENESS!

I personally KNOW that PHYSICAL FITNESS should be as important in your SITUATION AWARENESS, PREPAREDNESS and SURVIVAL training. It is at the top of the list for our US Special Forces. One of the most intense fitness programs in the military is the legendary Navy SEALS training and Hell Week. Another of my mentors is former US Navy SEAL Commander Mark Divine, who runs SEALFit, Unbeatable Mind and the Kokoro Challenge, which is a civilian version of SEAL Hell Week.

Have you heard of CrossFit? Greg Amundson, author of the best selling *Firebreather Fitness* and *God In Me*, has become a close friend. Greg has had an amazing career beginning as a deputy sheriff, continuing as a captain in the US Army MPs (my Dad was Military Police for the legendary General George Patton) and then joining the DEA. His latest venture is seminary school! Greg is one of the pioneers of CrossFit.

Next comes MENTAL FITNESS. Are you aware that the US military is now teaching meditation, mindfulness, and other stress reducing abilities? One of the Special Forces that are taking this to another level are the US Army Rangers. Here is what was said in the May 2017 issue of *Men's Health*:

"Heinz (he is the Ranger's mental coach) and Noble (he is a PhD Ranger captain and 2nd Battalion 75th Regiment psychologist) work constantly to make Rangers mentally tougher, emphasizing the big picture as well as in-the-moment strategies. The Rangers are moving away from goal-setting and instead focusing on 'being'.

"Are you the person you want to be? How are you working towards that? What is stopping you from being that person?"

Rangers are now about forging a sense of PURPOSE and WARRIOR MINDSET!

This is what we want for you in this book! You need to find YOUR purpose and warrior mindset like my ancestors the Scottish Knights Templars did!

Next let's move on to PREPAREDNESS. The Scouts have the right motto: BE PREPARED and I would only add AT ALL TIMES!

It is a FULL TIME 365/24/7 commitment for REAL preparedness! You must KNOW what to do in numerous scenarios as we teach at [Templar Commandos](http://www.templarcommandos.com) for teens 13-19 and their parents and [XtremePreparedness](http://www.xtremepreparedness.com) Commandos boot camps.

BY the way pay NO attention to those preparedness and survival reality TV shows. They are TOTAL RUBBISH! I am a certified Comcast TV producer and have been producing video and TV shows since the mid-1980s!

First real producers have to storyboard the entire 48 minutes of an hour TV show! When I was a reporter for both CBS News and Post Newsweek TV we had a director in the studio booth, who had received a copy of what the assignment editor had scripted! Same today! SCRIPTED!

For instance on the popular TV series *Survivor*, they may be on an island but when someone is kicked off they return to a nice comfy hotel room on that island! I will assure you with three TV crews working eight hour shifts around the clock, these guys are NOT going to be staying in a tent! When their shift is over they head for the hotel!

Yes it will be very difficult for the last few survivors, who have probably been on that island for at least a month. That is why they are paid the BIG bucks!

Now for what I call Prepper type preparedness. Most of the Preppers I have seen are overweight out-of-shape SLOBS, who haven't seen past their waist line in years! They also think because they have 1500 canned goods in a basement that they are PREPARED! Yes it is nice to have the food and water barrels ready but that is NOT the type of PREPAREDNESS we will be teaching you!

What gets me are these STUPID PREPPERS that go on a Prepper TV show and SHOW and TELL people their PREPAREDNESS!

I have a professional team that could pull up in a "moving van" from the neighbor's point of because we have just that day stenciled it on the truck! Most are so UNAWARE that they would never notIce as we picked the easy lock on the door! Even if they did ask us we could be as convincing as Hollywood actors telling them we had permission!

Next we would head for their basement and begin hauling off those canned goods and other preparedness supplies especially their weapons and electronics. Even if we had to enter a yard with vicious watch dogs we could tranquillize them!

The most likely scenario that we want you to AVOID AT ALL COST is opening your big mouth to brag about your preparedness! This is between you and your family – NO ONE ELSE! When everything goes down, the LAST thing you want is people knowing about your preparedness and supplies. Then they are going to know where to go to get FREE supplies for their family!

KEEP YOUR MOUTH SHUT! My Templar ancestors had already figured out that King Philipe of France wanted the Templar wealth in our Paris treasury. They had SECRETLY planned to get it out long before King Philipe arrived! Ditto for the London treasury!

They kept their mouths SHUT!

You and your family should have a SAFE AREA to retreat to at least 100 miles from an urban area. Again do NOT tell any of your friends (unless they are TRUSTED ones participating in the experience) about this SAFE AREA! If you are not able to have one, then you will need several plans for hunkering down at home for up to 6 MONTHS! That is why all my clients have 6 months of preparedness supplies at all times!

At XtremePreparedness we are the first that will be offering for sale online our COMPLETE ECO-VILLAGE packages that you will learn more about later in the book! Also we will be building one you will see in the western North Carolina mountains in 2018!

There will most likely be chaos and panic especially if it is an act of terrorism effecting the entire USA i.e. taking down the power grid. I have written another book *Grid Going Down!* available on Amazon. The more likely scenario here in the USA will be the overpowering of our grid with all the gigantic HDTV screens, kitchen appliances, toys, etc. It will most likely cause what is known as the Domino Effect across the USA leaving us in darkness, powering off all the ATMs, forcing all the stores to close, shutting off all the gas at service stations, etc.

So first thing you do is keep a 6 month supply of BATTERIES on hand at all times! I even have: a portable solar panel that fits in my backpack; a SunOven™ for cooking, baking, broiling, boiling and dehydrating; and 400 watt Crank-A-Watt™ for powering small appliances.

This the type of PREPAREDNESS we teach our clients and hopefully you and your family.

One of the MUST items that will be discussed in depth later is a BUG-OUT BACKPACK! It should be with you at ALL times weighing in at about 20 pounds.

If it became necessary, you and your family might have to leave your urban area preferably on mountain bikes but possibly by foot. Even at 71 years young I could hike 20 miles a day with my backpack!

Could YOU? Now do you see why FITNESS is so important!

What we will be teaching you here could lead to your SURVIVAL! You have to be SITUATIONALLY AWARE. You have to be PHYSICALLY and MENTALLY fit. Finally you have got to be PREPARED!

My Templar ancestors SURVIVED because of this MINDSET! Very few were tortured and burned at the stake. Over 20,000 escaped from France and went to what is today known as SWITZERLAND! They had SECRETLY PREPARED for what became Friday 13th as we even celebrate today with Black Friday sales, horror movies, parties, etc.

The last thing I want to discuss with you in this Introduction is why I have subtitled this book: **BE PREPARED NOT SCARED!.**

Currently I estimate there are only TWO PERCENT of Americans that are at as I have coined - the XTREMEPREPAREDNESS level!

TWO PERCENT!

My goal in writing this book is to move it to THREE PERCENT or another 3,000,000 plus Americans who take what I am sharing here and become SELF RELIANT as opposed to expecting government in the form of first responders to take care of you!

It ain't going to HAPPEN! I have many first responders as friends as law enforcement officers, fire fighting personnel and EMTS. They have told me they are not paid enough to stand on the streets during these disasters we see as possible in the future! They will be going to SAFE AREAS with their loved ones!

This is NOT to instill F.E.A.R. in you! This is just a FACT!

I realized that I could have been instilling F.E.A.R. into readers with my previous books.

So what is F.E.A.R.?

One of my mentors the late Foster Hibbard coined this word which stands for FALSE EVIDENCE APPEARING REAL!

There is NO evidence that Preparedness and Survival should instill FEAR into you!

What has been the Boy Scouts motto since the beginning?

BE PREPARED!

Are you READY? Then read on!

NOTES:

CHAPTER 1
Situational Awareness

First thanks to the IDIOTS here at Word I lost this entire chapter when I went to copy and paste! You would think that after all the years Microsoft has been in business they would have a system that is FOOL PROOF like WordPress for saving revisions! Even the Vice President of Word said there was NO way to recover my previous work using my Apple iPad mini I write my books on! I would NEVER trust any Microsoft product as those that bought their Surface tablets are learning!

Enough ranting let's get on with why I put so much emphasis on SITUATIONAL AWARENESS.

Today the only thing MOST people are aware of is their smartphone as I mentioned before.

In fact numerous cases of recent carjacking have been contributed to not being in a state of SITUATIONAL AWARENESS!

Criminals and terrorists are VERY SITUATIONALLY AWARE! Are you?

Recently I have been reading a fascinating book entitled *Deep Survival* by adventurer Laurence Gonzales, who has spent decades learning from experts and his own harrowing experiences he puts himself through about why the majority of us do NOT survive!

He delves into the mind and the brain that sets up what he calls "emotional markers and mental maps" that instead of helping us during a survival scenario can get us injured and killed! For instance, a 20 year veteran US Army Ranger was doing a simple raft down the West Virginia Gauley River with a river guide. Even on less dangerous rivers rafters have been known to be flipped out of the raft. That is what happened to this Ranger. When the guide got the raft ready to continue down the river, he went to help this Ranger back on the raft. It is reported the Ranger laughed and turned down the guide's offer deciding to FLOAT DOWN THE RIVER as Rangers and my mentor Tom Brown were taught. You flip over on your back with your feet pointed where you are going. This is exactly what the Ranger did.

Unfortunately this trained veteran Ranger DROWN in less than THREE FEET of water when he encountered a rock blocking the middle of the current. He was sucked under the water, became pinned and drown!

Surely you would expect a well fed, not sleepy, alert Ranger veteran would have easily survived?

Why didn't he survive?

Gonzales says that the "mental map" of a US Army Ranger especially a 20 year veteran probably is what got him killed! Here is what Gonzales says: "...in Ranger culture, having to be rescued is IGNOMINIOUS (my emphasis). It is associated with a bad outcome: SHAME, FAILURE (my emphasis). In Ranger training, if you have to be rescued, you are

OUT OF THE PROGRAM (my emphasis). The emotional bookmarks that Gabba (last name of deceased Ranger) developed had labeled rescue as BAD (my emphasis) and self-sufficiency and even pain as GOOD (my emphasis), no matter how threatening the environment...Death before DISHONOR (my emphasis). Rangers lead the way, they don't follow."

Gonzales goes on to give many tragic examples of so called experts and experienced adventurers being seriously hurt or killed because of their EMOTIONAL MARKERS and MENTAL MAPS.

Too many even SITUATIONALLY AWARE individuals, who have had YEARS of training and experience are victims because the MENTAL MAP changed during that particular scenario. For instance, it could be a higher altitude than climbed before. It could be a not expected quick change in weather conditions. It could be higher waves than one has surfed before. The CHANGES are ENDLESS!

So how do you avoid being hurt or killed in CHANGING situations?

Gonzales concludes that you have to BE HERE NOW! This is exactly what SITUATIONAL AWARENESS experts like myself teach! Be PRESENT at ALL times if possible. If you find yourself lost, get into the PRESENT! Look at the time on your watch to determine if the sun is going down BEFORE you could hopefully backtrack to your starting destination! If so, consider doing what we teach our clients – either find a make-do shelter or build one!

This especially applies if you are in a high location or during a cold (even cool!) time of the year! Get yourself WARM and stay DRY! Of course I ALWAYS have something with me at ALL times that allows me to create a make-do shelter. Preferably if I have my Bug-Out backpack, I have the Lawson hammock/tent combo weighing in about two pounds!

Remember this VERY important information that is NOT internet myth: 3 MINUTES before you will need OXYGEN; 3 DAYS before you will need WATER and 3 WEEKS before you will need FOOD!

So in the above scenario with the sun going down, you are NOT going to have to worry to much about these 3s! My clients are most likely going to be rescued before 3 days! Any way we outfit them with the Sawyer Water Filtration kit that can filter up to 100,000 gallons and easily fits in the smallest backpack! Also we have them add the Sawyer Sting and Bite kit for insects and snakes!

To make it easier we also encourage them to carry our Survivor Industries 3 days of FOOD AND WATER packets. Again easy to fit into the smallest backpack!

So I hope you are getting the message loud and clear how you need to be prepared with SITUATIONAL AWARENESS for your particular adventure you are planning! For instance, if my client is going beyond three days, I want him/her carrying another 3 days of the food and water packets. Also I teach them that since they can survive without ANY WATER for 3 days they should conserve its usage if they find they have not been found within 24 hours! I can almost

GUARANTEE if they follow what we pound into their heads they will be found within 24 hours on US soil! Of course weather conditions could increase the time factor!

AND most importantly we tell them to STAY RIGHT WHERE THEY ARE! Do NOT try to go forward especially if there is a large tract of wilderness close by! With what they are carrying they can easily without a great deal of STRESS SURVIVE!

As I mentioned before one of my mentors is one of the most SITUATIONALLY AWARE individuals in the world – TOM BROWN!

So let's begin to find what Tom has taught thousands of individuals like yourself about SITUATIONAL AWARENESS in NATURE! Remember he is the premiere tracker of animals and also humans on this Planet!

When you head out for a FULL-OUT ADVENTURE in NATURE - CLEAR YOUR MIND!

We have our students SIT down and get STILL and then we teach them BOX BREATHING which I learned from another mentor, former Navy SEAL Commander Mark Divine in his Kokoro Yoga Challenge. You learn to breathe from your BELLY as I have done most of the past 40 years after taking Hatha Yoga from the same teacher that worked with The Beatles.

I find the best way to observe BELLY BREATHING is to LAY DOWN on your BACK and put your HAND on your BELLY.

As you breathe IN feel your BELLY RISING and then as you breathe OUT feel it LOWERING.

Why not practice this RIGHT NOW and build up to where you can do this for 5 minutes at a time.

Next it is time to move onto what Commander Mark Divine and his daughter Catherine teach - BOX BREATHING!

Here is what you are going to do:

1. Breathe IN as you did before with a DEEP BELLY breath so that you feel your BELLY EXPANDING as you place your HAND on it. COUNT 1001, 1002, 1003 and 1004.
2. Now I want you to HOLD that for a count of FOUR - 1001, 1002, 1003 and 1004.
3. Now let it out SLOWLY for a count of 1001, 1002, 1003, and 1004.
4. AND HOLD for 1001, 1002, 1003 and 1004 NOT breathing!
5. REPEAT #1.

That's it! By the way the reason you count this way is because each 1001, 1002, 1003, and 1004 count is close to ONE SECOND.

You are now doing BOX BREATHING!

Try to build up to 5 MINUTES and you will REALLY notice a DIFFERENCE!

Here are some more tips that Tom says helps when you are out in nature:

1. Let go of time! Take off your watch and SHUT OFF your cell phone!

2. SLOW DOWN and SEE, LISTEN, SMELL and TOUCH nature!
3. Let go of WORRIES! That is why we teach the BOX BREATHING so you will get STILL!
4. Be QUIET! Keep talking to an absolute MINIMUM! Remember animals pick up real easily on humans talking!
5. Don't ANALYZE just ENJOY! As Tom so aptly puts it: "Know the SOUL before you know the name."
6. NOTHING is COMMON PLACE! Each moment in nature is a NEW one!
7. Let your HEART be your guide! Leave your INHIBITIONS somewhere else!
8. And mine - EXPERIENCE XTREMEJOY!

Tom also says that when you IMMERSE yourself in NATURE you should set NO LIMITS.

For instance, if you are near a swamp JUMP IN! Get dirty, smelly and wet!

For me I don't think that is going to happen! Of course for YOU coming to one of our boot camps that could DEFINITELY happen!

Second become a CHILD again!

Have you ever watched a child out in NATURE?

When I was a leader for the heart warming Sierra Club Inner City Outings program in Atlanta I saw these young inner city kids eyes light up as soon as we entered the trail! They had NEVER seen anything like this spending their entire lives in a rat infested, scary, crime ridden inner city ghetto! Sure they were frighten but they were more EXCITED and JOYFUL!

Become like these kids - EXCITED and full of XTREMEJOY!

Now we begin to study how we use our FIVE SENSES habitually and how we can change this!

Tom says that we become HABITUAL in the way we see things. For instance when we go out into our yard we see the spring flowers the way we have always seen them - usually from afar!

Tom says: "To see the world from ever-new vantage points is one of the most basic lessons in nature observation. Whenever you are out in nature, vary your angle of vision. Don't just walk along with your eyes on the ground ahead. Look up, down, sideways, and back. Look where you are going, but also look where you're not going. Most important, explore places you would normally not go and look at things in ways you would normally not see them."

So with those spring flowers look CLOSER at them. Look from ABOVE like a bird or bee would. Look from BELOW like an ant might!

Here is a SEEING exercise that both Tom and I teach.

I learned this in my two years of studying Ninjutsu with Sensei Bud Malmstrom.

Animals have EXCELLENT PERIPHERAL vision while we usually do not.

However as Sensei taught us YOU can develop it with this exercise:

1. Stand nice and straight with your HANDS AND ARMS out straight in front of you with the PALMS turned INSIDE with a distance of about SHOULDER width.
2. Now begin to SLOWLY expand your hands and arms OUT until they are lined up with your SHOULDERS. As you SLOWLY expand KEEPING your HEAD looking STRAIGHT AHEAD see how far you can still see the TIPS OF YOUR FINGERS.
3. When you have expanded to line up with your SHOULDERS wiggle your FINGERS? Can you see them?
4. If so, continue to expand SLOWLY beyond your SHOULDERS wiggling your FINGERS until you can NOT see them. When you can not see them then this is the LIMIT of your CURRENT PERIPHERAL VISION!
5. Keep practicing until you CAN see BEYOND your SHOULDERS!

Tom adds another exercise this time seeing how far you can see on a VERTICAL level.

1. Put your HANDS together with PALMS FACING EACH OTHER at SHOULDER height.
2. Now begin to EXPAND them UP and DOWN SLOWLY until you can NOT see them.

These exercises could SAVE your LIFE one day!

Once you have learned these exercises, you can begin to develop what Tom calls SPLATTER VISION.

I learned this in my Ninja training and what you are doing is "softening" your focus and WIDENING your view to take in at least the distance you developed when you spread out your hands to SHOULDER width and wiggled your fingers. For most of you that is about 180 degrees.

Here is why Tom says you need SPLATTER VISION: "The earth and sky may be filled with movements you have not noticed before. The environment may seem more alive...Whatever you see, it should be more than you noticed before, because you will have multiplied you ability to detect movement by several HUNDRED PERCENT (my emphasis).

"Walk through the woods with your head up and your eyes on the horizon. As you walk, direct your attention to the edges of your vision. Try to pick up things that are passing on the outermost fringes-trees, bushes, logs, etc. Then notice that, without moving your head or your eyes, you can be aware of almost anything in your field of vision just by choosing to see it!...It's a little like watching a movie, being aware of everything on the screen of your mind. This is SPLATTER VISION at its best."

Keep exercising your SPLATTER VISION by slipping in and out of it at frequent intervals!

Tom teaches us how to observe as if we were at ANT level!

This will require you to eventually get DOWN as close to ANT level as possible.

1. Mark off with twigs or string an area 12 inches by 12 inches. It does not matter where you do this.

2. Stand up and OBSERVE what you see in that marked off area. Most likely you are not going to see very much.

3. Now SIT down as close to your marked off area as possible. Now I want you to sit like that OBSERVING ONLY your marked off area for at least 5 MINUTES! I will bet you that as you FOCUS on just this marked off square you are going to begin to see much more than standing up! I would advise you move your FOCUS from one area of the square to another every minute.

4. Finally you are going to LAY DOWN as close to your marked off area as possible for at least another 5 MINUTES. Again FOCUS on a different area of the square for at least a minute.

You are going to be amazed at what you have been missing!

We did this at one of my Sierra Club workshops and it was AWESOME!

You looked at a 12 INCH SQUARE and now we are going to learn to EXPAND that view.

Tom suggest you get yourself a camera. Your cell phone one should do.

Great photographers like my friend Paul Faso, the Official Limited Edition photographer for the 1986 Statue of Liberty Celebration learn to find interesting ways to shoot the ORDINARY like the Statue of Liberty you see below.

So get your camera out and start taking photos of ORDINARY nature from EXTRAORDINARY ways!

Here is another exercise that Tom suggests for studying NATURE that does NOT require a camera:

"When you see something you want to concentrate on, look at it through the hole created by curling your index finger. Move your 'lens' around, trying to create interesting patterns. Look at small things close up. Examine surfaces, textures, patterns – whatever interest you. Looking through this narrow 'viewfinder' not only concentrates your focus, but cuts all confusing elements in your peripheral vision. It forces you to look at familiar things outside of their usual context."

We have discussed SPLATTER VISION, CAMERA VISION and now MICROSCOPIC VISION.

No you do not need to bring a microscope with you but a 4X MAGNIFYING GLASS will be perfect for this exercise which is playing as if you are an ANT looking at a LEAF! You will want to get down on the ground and look closely at the veins in the leaf. Also look at the different colors of the leaf. Look at it from different angles. See what the ANT is seeing!

Tom discusses how he loves to see how an artist SEES nature with all its color, shadows, textures, and lighting. Then he goes to the place the artist did the painting to see what the artist has MISSED.

Here is what he says in his book entitled *Field Guide to Nature Observation and Tracking* (available at Resources at my SituationalAwareness.Expert (http://www.situationalawareness.expert) :

"Until we tag names and values onto specific objects, we see everything purely. We cannot tell shadow from substance or color from texture. Everything is seen as a marvelous collage."

Now you can begin to see things with the eye of an artist!

Tom further says: "Next time you look at a familiar scene, blot out the context in which you usually see it. Blur your eyes a bit and forget the objects themselves. Look instead for shadows, shapes, textures, colors, and lighting."

I love this quote from one of my heroes Henry David Thoreau from his classic *Walden*:

"If you are ready to leave father and mother, and brother and sister, and wife and children and friends, and NEVER (my emphasis) see them again – if you have paid your debts, and made your will, and settled all your affairs, and are a free man, then you are READY (my emphasis) for a walk."

IN NATURE!

Returning to watching nature as Tom Brown has been teaching us, we now explore COLOR in nature.

Tom says not to try to see the scene of the forest but only the COLORS separately. See the different COLORS especially their richness and variety. Next pick ONE COLOR like green and see the different shades of green in the forest. Artists have different names for this like warm, cold, light, dark, bland, metallic, earthy, etc. See if you can see these different attributes of green or the color you chose.

Artists and photographers know the importance of LIGHT in a painting or photograph. So experience your color as you would see it at sunrise and throughout the day until sunset.

As Tom says: "You will see shapes loom into light or disappear into darkness, colors brighten or blend, shadows grow or fade, and textures deepen or flatten."

Now we move from SEEING to LISTENING to nature.

Right now wherever you are I want you to sit QUIETLY and listen to what you are hearing.

Right now in my apartment I am hearing the ticking of the wall clock, the hum of the fridge, the tapping of my fingers over the keyboard, the snap crackle and pop of my neck, and I think the rain falling on the roof.

So as soon as you can I want you to go OUTSIDE, if you are not already there. I want you to again sit quietly for at least 15 MINUTES and LISTEN CLOSELY.

Are you hearing birds chirping, dogs barking, vehicles, people talking, etc.?

These would be the NORMAL sounds you hear. I want to you to OPEN UP your ears to other sounds like the wind moving through the leaves, the grass crackling as an insect moves through it, possibly a mouse running close by, etc. These are the SUBTLE sounds most of us miss when we don't FOCUS on LISTENING!

If you did this in your backyard next time try doing it in a nearby park.

Remember before we learned to SEE as artists and now we are going to learn to HEAR as a musician.

Here is what you are going to want to hear while sitting besides a rushing stream of water: its tone, pitch and rhythm it makes. Also it is not a single sound as Tom points out but: "a symphony of sounds." He further says: "Within the overall rush, listen to the water also gurgling, flowing, seeping, splattering, and dripping."

You can do same with the rain, wind, birds, animals, etc.

Tom tells how you can FOCUS on different sounds of nature.

Take you thumb and index finger and cup them around your ear. Then move your ear around.

You will be amazed how sounds that were just barely audible become clearer.

We are one of the only mammals that have ears that do NOT move around towards the sounds automatically.

Continuing about SOUND and LISTENING, Tom says that to zero in on a sound you should first cup your ears as described above and then move say your left one up and your right one down. Next take both hands and cup the ear that is presenting the sound the LOUDEST. Now you should be able to PINPOINT the source of the sound!

He also tells of how his mentor Stalking Wolf would tell him a snake was down by the river when they were NOT even near the river!

How did Stalking Wolf know?

He was not psychic; however he knew the SOUNDS of other animals and birds would make when a snake was in the vicinity!

Here is what Tom says: "As an Indian scout, Stalking Wolf knew that nothing happens that does not affect everything else, that every animal sends ripples of reaction through the other residents in its neighborhood just like a rock thrown into water sends concentric waves to the far corners of a pond."

And speaking about a rock, Tom says that if you put your ear close to a rock or hollow tree stump you will have sounds also amplified as these act as ECHO CHAMBERS.

Now we move into SMELL as we renew our senses in nature.

Tom says and he is right that we have desensitized our sense of SMELL especially as we enter nature.

Tom says: "…the wilderness is a veritable treasure chest of aromas. The perfumes of wild flowers, the dank, musty scent of earth, the sweet smell of evergreen needles, the cool freshness of water – there are endless combinations of molecules dancing in the air, each with the signatures of animals, plants, and minerals that produced them."

So here is an exercise to get you back to using your sense of SMELL.

Breathe through your nose and at the same time FEEL the air moving through your nostrils. In addition to the smells around you, Tom says to sense the temperature and humidity in the air.

Go SMELL nature RIGHT NOW!

Tom suggest taking a group of items and determining how they smell compared to each other. Examples would be a lemon, orange, banana, peanut butter, bark, grass, clothing, perfume, deodorant, dirt, etc.

Now close your eyes and begin to SMELL starting with the strongest one i.e. perfume or the lemon and working your way to the weakest smelling one which might be clothing.

Another exercise he suggest when you are out in nature is to gather up wild growing items like the leaf of a plant or a strip of bark of a tree, a flower, etc. Collect as many as you can. Again close your eyes and SMELL. Then after each item open your eyes and see which one it was. The more often you do this, the more likely you will be like your pooch that goes wild when you roll down the window to allow the odors to permeate the atmosphere around the dog!

Finally start doing this as Tom suggest: "Each time you find a den, burrow, or other animal indicator, get down and smell it. How would you characterize the odor? Is it musty, pungent, weak, sharp, or noxious? Is it strange or familiar? Can you identify the animal that left the smell?"...Make this exercise a long term habit. As you progress, you will begin to understand just how critical a nature observation and tracking device the nose really is."

Next we look at TOUCHING THE EARTH!

Tom suggests you go out into nature BLINDFOLDED (of course with a partner!) and begin to FEEL different items like rocks, flowers, trees, moving water, leaves, moss, grass, etc. You're going to be searching for different TEXTURES – smooth, rough, slimy, etc. Also you are going to want to notice the TEMPERATURE of these different objects – cool, warm, cold, hot, etc.

Yes you can do this with ANIMALS but it would probably be better to do this NOT blindfolded and may be at a petting zoo or county fair. I remember that as a kid we would spend our Thanksgiving day at Ocala, Florida, where the famous Ross Allen Animal & Reptile Farm was also located at near by Silver Springs. They would allow you to touch the snakes. One that I volunteered to TOUCH was a VERY large sleek black boa constrictor!

Now I bet you thought it would be slimy!

WRONG! It was like having SILK wrapped around you! I was literally holding its head with one hand and the tail with the other with the rest of this snake wrapped around me! Fortunately he or she had been trained not to constrict around volunteers like me!

I am a fanatic about HORSES and ha stepped on, thrown, bucked and even nipped tell you each species of horse had a different feeling coat!

Next let's move to TASTE!

Here is where you need to be EXTREMELY CAREFUL with TASTING nature! If you don't know your WILD EDIBLES (you should put that on your "bucket list"!), then don't taste particularly MUSHROOMS as you could become VERY ill or DIE!

Here are several videos that I shot about WILD EDIBLES with first PATRICIA HOWELL, a world renowned expert and author with a 6 month waiting list for her workshops:

Patricia Howell (https://youtu.be/oRlUHon4hlQ)

I was also fortunate to meet a cool dude driving a hippie VW van that I named Nature Boy Doug, who also is an expert on WILD EDIBLES:

Video 1 (https://youtu.be/GRloiizq0i4)

Video 2 (https://youtu.be/Y13XIhih1hA)

Video 3 (https://youtu.be/fb7pSa5rEcI)

Video 4 (https://youtu.be/0U7SOuWmGRw)

Video 5 (https://youtu.be/znQLAzBKvEY)

Well we have ended our chapter on SITUATIONAL AWARENESS out in nature! You have learned ways to experience SEEING, HEARING, SMELLING, TASTING and TOUCHING especially if you have watched the videos with experts Patricia and Nature Boy Doug.

These exercises that you should have done can help you even with urban SITUATIONAL AWARENESS and could save your life or loved ones and friends!

Next we are going to move into URBAN SITUATIONAL AWARENESS.

NOTES:

CHAPTER 2

Urban Situational Awareness

The majority of you are going to face scenarios involving URBAN ones as opposed to ones in rural areas. Even if you live in a small rural town like I do, you can benefit from what I am going to share.

First ALL the exercises in the previous chapter especially the ones with VISION and HEARING could help you in an urban scenario.

First as mentioned earlier, your WORST enemy is going to be that SMARTPHONE! And it does not apply to youngsters either. I see seniors every day with their attention riveted to that damn little smartphone screen! They are either texting while driving (BIG NO NO!) or doing social media on Facebook (I get my clients off this app as quick as possible!), Twitter, SnapChat, LinkedIn, Periscope, Instagram, YouTube, etc. THEY ARE NOT SITUATIONALLY AWARE! Also they are the ones targeted in most scenarios I will be sharing!

Let me give you one scenario that is happening more and more every day in the USA – VEHICLE JACKING!

Want to know how to AVOID it?

This could be worth the money you paid for this book!

Here is how it happens.

You pull into a convenience store to get gas. You exit the vehicle and begin the gas pumping routine. Most of you think this is good time to see who has been texting you, catch up on social media, or even talk to someone on the smartphone.

WRONG!

You see vehicle jackers are usually working in pairs. One moves close to you and may even ask you a simple innocent question or usually try to panhandle you. Either way their job is to DISTRACT you even if you are NOT on the smartphone! While that is happening the other member is unhooking the hose from your gas tank and quickly moving towards the driver's seat.

Many of you are STUPID enough to even leave the engine running with the key in the ignition! This makes it real easy for the thief! Even if you did not leave the key in the ignition, this thief is real good at QUICK hot wiring the vehicle!

So now he signals his accomplice to get ready for the final phase of the operation – taking off and burning rubber as YOUR vehicle leaves the area!

Oh and most likely the one that has distracted you will push you down before jumping in the driver's seat which his/her accomplice has vacated to make it easier to make the get-a-way!

So after you have even gotten up, your vehicle will be on the street blending into the traffic!

How many of you think you could CORRECTLY tell the arriving officer your TAG NUMBER or even describe your CORRECT COLOR, MAKE, MODEL and YEAR of your vehicle much less any DISTINGUISHING marks like a dent on the right side or a For Sale sign in the rear window (most likely the AWARE criminals will see it!).

So how do you avoid this frightening scenario?

First when you get out of your vehicle, stay FOCUSED on putting the hose in the vehicle and STAND BY it at ALL times! If someone tries to distract you from what you are are FOCUSED on doing IGNORE them! 90 times out of 100 a potential vehicle jacker will realize you are NOT a good target and wait for another UNAWARE motorist! Also if you are LOCKED AND LOADED with the gun showing (my preferred way!) they will definitely wait for another victim! If you have to do this late at night be damn sure you are ARMED especially if you are a female!

If you MUST go into the convenience store, get the key out of the ignition if you have not already done that and then LOCK the vehicle! It astounds me how many STUPID people go into the store leaving the vehicle UNLOCKED!

Here is one I bet you NEVER thought of. Take photos of each of your vehicles on your smartphone! One of the back with the TAG NUMBER. The second of the front with the TAG NUMBER if your state requires it. The third of the LEFT side of the vehicle especially of IDENTIFYING marks. Ditto for the RIGHT side photo.

Now when the arriving officer ask you about the vehicle you will have photos of it!

By the way with my SITUATIONAL AWARENESS app I discussed above, it would be possible for the victim to post the photos of the hijacked vehicle long before the cops arrived on the scene!

As I write this book we are approaching the time thieves love the most – CHRISTMAS!

Let' see what you should be doing!

When we are running a security detail with a client we ALWAYS use three members MINIMUM!

One is on point at the TOP of our protection triangle and out FRONT of our client/s. Two are located in the BACK at the BASE of the triangle with the client/s in the MIDDLE of the triangle. The detail is CLOSE enough to prevent a potential kidnapping but far enough away in the back and front to even look like they are protecting the client/s.

When you see these big burly dudes surrounding the Hollywood star that is TOTAL BS and these IDIOTS are clueless on what should be really done! Of course they may really know they are screwing up protection but the EGO MANIAC client wants people to know they are there! What MORONS!

When I met my Chief Security Officer, Tim, a former UK Royal Marine Commando and Special Boat Services (equivalent to our US Navy SEALs) I was actually kind of taken back. Tim being as astute as he is said: "What were you expecting, mate, Rambo?"

Tim is in great shape but far from the muscle bound ones you see protecting these Hollywood MORONS! And that is why he is so damn good at what he and his former UK Special Forces mates do – NOT STAND OUT!

He is the one who taught me the the three point system I just described. He also said that many times the woman with the children is another member of the detail! Hollywood Moms on an outing with their kids face not only the asshole paparazzi but potential kidnappers!

Okay so how can you as a Dad out with the family protect them in the mall or at an event?

First teach the kids to STAY CLOSE BY and not dart around like most of the brats I see!

Dad should be in the BACK of his family and he should at ALL TIMES be using his peripheral vision training he learned above! He should NOT be concerned with what is being touted in the windows even if it is something he is drawn to! Keep looking left and right and even up if there is a second floor! Stay in SITUATIONAL AWARENESS mode!

Hey you Moms out there you need to put one kid on your LEFT and another one on your RIGHT and tell them to stay next to you at ALL TIMES! If you have more than two to guard, then consider getting a frIend to go with you to watch the other ones! Or better yet get a TRUSTED male friend to first read my book and second practice SITUATIONAL AWARENESS as I describe here.

Here is one particularly for you ladies especially if you are alone.

You are going to be parking your vehicle either outside or in a parking garage. Perfect opportunity for thieves to assault you and steal the vehicle! Again PAY ATTENTION to the SURROUNDINGS as you exit. Again especially if you are alone, be LOCKED AND LOADED! Let any lingering asshole see the gun and your menacing look of – BACK OFF ASSHOLE!

Next you want to take a photo of the AISLE NUMBER you are parked on! Believe me there have been times I have exited from the vehicle in the past thinking I would EAISLY find it on my return!

WRONG!

Ditto for the FLOOR NUMBER you are parked on in the parking garage.

So now you are loaded down with packages and decide it is time to take a food court break. Frankly during the Holiday Season I would not advise eating at the food court. Splurge on an INSIDE restaurant!

Okay let's say you are hot for one of the food court meals. You got your arms loaded down with packages and you are trying to pay the vendor from your purse. Believe me a potential thief is seeing your antics and realizing you could be the perfect one to ROB!

You can only find a seat near the traffic lanes in the mall.

NEVER sit there!

Why?

Remember that thief watching you back at the vendor? Now he or she knows that most likely you are NOT going to place your packages UNDER the seat area by your feet, where you should! Also like 90% of the women I see you sling your purse over the back of the chair!

WRONG! Put your purse in your LAP!

Better yet check your packages at the concierge desk! Yes it might costs you something but I will assure you it will be a hell of a lot less than the Coach handbag you just treated yourself to! With your bags checked SAFELY you can enjoy that food court lunch without keeping an eye on every passerby that could be targeting you!

So now you are finished with your shopping.

Most likely you have at least several packages and you might even have several kids tagging along in the worse case scenario. If they have also eaten at the food court, they most likely got some sweet treat and now their blood sugar is starting to lead to hyper activity. Or they are spoiled brats that are whining that you did not buy them the toy they seem to think they are entitled to before Santa arrives!

Either way with or without kids I will bet you that you are STRESSED OUT like the majority of those shopping especially during the Holidays! If you have forgotten to take a photo of the aisle or floor you are parked on, that will mean more wasted STRESSFUL time looking for your vehicle with your hands and arms loaded with packages! Add screaming or whiny kids and the STRESS level should be through the roof!

Finally you find your vehicle. You decide to put your packages in the trunk.

WRONG!

More people are robbed and even seriously injured while opening their trunk to put in packages! Here is what happen to a friend of mine formerly of the CIA. Now you would have thought Harry would have known better especially in Miami! He comes out of the grocery store and opens his trunk. Places the groceries in the trunk. As he is beginning to pull his body and head out of the trunk, a thief slams the trunk lid down on Harry. Rips his REAL Rolex off his wrist! He could have cared less about Harry's groceries!

Same could happen to our STRESSED OUT lady putting her packages in her trunk! The thief could have been watching what she had been purchasing including that expensive Coach handbag. Also she could be like STUPID Harry wearing a REAL luxury watch and or diamond bracelet!

This is NOT the time to wear ANY jewelry or watches that look even expensive! Best yet don't wear any jewelry!

So how do you avoid this potential disaster?

Remember the concierge desk? Don't get your packages UNTIL they can bring them out to your vehicle! Go to your vehicle EMPTY HANDED!

Well not exactly empty handed!

I want you to take out your key ring hopefully with MACE attached like I do. I want you to take your LONGEST keys and put one in between each finger. Then make a tight fist. You want to make sure ANY potential thief sees this maneuver! I grant you he/she will think twice before approaching you!

Just make your shopping trip as LESS STRESSFUL as possible!

Of course I'm telling our clients to do as much shopping as possible ONLINE! Over 90% of my shopping even in my little western North Carolina town is now with AMAZON and WISH! Sure I will go out to my fairly safe WallyWorld or Kmart occasionally. However I have even done shopping on their online site! Buy it there and have it delivered to either my UPS Store or the store itself.

I particularly love that if I am not happy with my Amazon purchase, I can return it to my UPS Store and my refund is IMMEDIATELY back in my account!

No standing in line with other STRESSED OUT people who are returning items!

We have discussed shopping but what about going to events like concerts and ball games?

Again you have to be in the same exact SITUATIONAL AWARENESS mode as you were when shopping! My buddy Dave, a concealed weapons proponent, carries his 40 caliber with him to these events. He has it right beside him as he is exiting the vehicle. Then he will open the trunk and place it in there.

Let me tell you what he told me. He and his girlfriend were attending a concert in Atlanta. He was returning from the concert when a girl approached him asking for a cigarette. Sounds INNOCENT enough. However DAVE being a TOTAL SITUATIONALLY AWARE individual has noticed several minutes before the girl was accompanied by a guy with a backpack. He could with his PERIPHERAL VISION see the dude lurking close by.

Dave politely told the girl he did not smoke. Then she asked him if he would give her some money. He said no. At the same time Dave was opening his trunk and getting his gun out - making sure the girl SAW it! She immediately scurried away with the dude telling him I'm sure about seeing the gun!

I advise my clients to be sure they are LOCKED AND LOADED when especially attending an event that will let them out late at night! Do like Dave!

Another place especially seniors are NOT alert is in their own home! Here are some ways to avoid home robberies or invasions.

Many time thieves will watch you go to your mailbox especially when they think you will be receiving a Social Security check. So NEVER have this check or any checks sent to your residence. Send it directly to your bank. Better yet do like I do – get a mailbox at your UPS Store! By the way unlike the post office, I'm able to put Suite ____ on my mail and it qualifies where a post office box wouldn't! Also there is NO chance of packages being stolen!

Here is a simple thing you can add to your home. Put a chair or bench on your front porch for placing packages. Better yet if you have a garage, drive in and shut the garage door ASAP! Then take out your packages.

Another problem is having shrubbery too close to the house's sides. Make sure there is at least a foot or more of the shrubbery cut back from the sides. Also install lights not only at the doors but on the sides of the house.

These suggestions are not only for seniors but EVERY one living in their home or condo. Even if you live in an apartment pass on these suggestions to the manager and or supervisor.

Here is another situation that everyone should be in SITUATIONAL AWARENESS mode – while jogging or walking for exercise. We have a number of seniors using our 7 mile greenway daily. Many jog or walk alone. They are doing this when very few people might be there to help them! Don't you follow their STUPIDITY! Make sure you do this with a companion especially if you are a senior…preferably YOUNGER!

Here is my own situation. I live within MY walking distance of downtown Franklin. I also have to walk along a four lane highway with speeding vehicles. Many of the asshole rednecks around here think it is funny to see how close they can come to hitting me!

That was the situation until I found a strong military expanding baton. Now as I walk I twirl it and even hold it as if it looks like an assault rifle pointing right at the oncoming traffic! All of sudden the vehicles are getting in the far left lane when they see me! The word is out that I'm one CRAZY SOB! Fine with me! By the way I'm trained with that baton just like my Dad was as a military police guard for the legendary World War Two General Patton.

That brings me to remind you – GET TRAINED with every weapon you use! One of mentors says you are not trained until you can hit the bullseye area with 100 rounds without a miss! With my SWAT styled 12 gauge shotgun that means 100 rounds each standing, kneeling, prone, etc. WITHOUT A MISS! Same with my Taurus 380 and my new Glock 19 4 Gen.

Well I am sure there many more SITUATIONAL AWARENESS scenarios! As a purchaser of this book you can find updates at my SituationalAwareness.Expert (http://www.situationalawareness.expert) website.

NOTES:

CHAPTER 3
Preparedness & Survival Mindset

Currently I estimate there are only TWO PERCENT of Americans that are at as I have coined - the XTREMEPREPAREDNESS level!

TWO PERCENT!

My goal in writing this book is to move it to THREE PERCENT or another 3,000,000 Americans like you.

Let me give you a WAKEUP CALL! I have spoken to numerous first responders from SWAT, fire personnel and EMTs. They tell me that they are not paid enough to be on the streets protecting YOU and your family! They will be leaving with their loved ones to go to their SAFE AREAS!

This is NOT to instill F.E.A.R. in you! This is just a FACT!

So what is F.E.A.R.?

One of my mentors the late Foster Hibbard coined this word which stands for FALSE EVIDENCE APPEARING REAL!

There is NO evidence that Preparedness and Survival should instill FEAR into you!

Do not the Boy Scouts have the motto: BE PREPARED?

So let's first begin this new book with how to develop a MINDSET that does not instill F.E.A.R.

(Again Microsoft Word screwed up my work! Don't rely on it! Use OPEN OFFICE or another app!)

One of my closest friends are Dr. Michael Duckett and his wife Leslie who are well known experts in neuroscience and the human brain writing the best selling *The Mental Codes* at Resources at my SituationalAwareness.Expert (http://www.situationalawareness.expert) .

One of their exercises is what is called the F.E.A.R. Run Down where you are going to use VISUALIZATION just like US Special Forces are taught:

1. Identify the F.E.A.R. Let's use a F.E.A.R. you can identify with.
2. Begin to write down step-by-step asking yourself: "If this F.E.A.R. was REAL, what would happen to me?"
3. After WRITING out the answers, ask yourself this important question: "If the next result happens to occur, what would happen next?" Remember you are usually writing down the WORST case scenario.
4. Now you are going to take each result that could occur and keep WRITING what could occur with each scenario getting worse.
5. When you have successfully finished this exercise, you will find that as Michael says: "You are still alive and this too shall pass." Actually, it could be a God given WAKEUP call!

Now that you have learned the Fear Run Down, I suggest you start making it a regular part of your training. Do Fear Run Downs on ALL the scenarios that you think apply to you in Situational Awareness, Preparedness and Survival.

Here are some more things that Michael and Lesley say about F.E.A.R:

"You can only succeed in any area of your life to the level of your greatest fear. Fear is a tether that holds you at a specific level of existence. Each time you attempt to expand beyond that point, you find yourself being pulled back to a stuck point."

Right now find a rubber band. Now take that band and pull it out from its current state. Now let it go. What happens? It returns to the state when you first encountered it. This is the "stuck point" the Ducketts refer to.

"You become ADDICTED (my emphasis) to the EMOTIONS (my emphasis) caused by your fears." Are you aware that the emotion caused by the F.E.A.R. is addictive like a drug? Depression according to the experts is really repressed anger, which of course is an emotion. Therefore depressed people actually become addicted to being depressed! It becomes a vicious cycle!

New research in EPIGENETICS (GOOGLE it!) says that not only do we become addicted but we more importantly can pass this on to children at birth!

During a Survival scenario this is LAST place you want to experience DEPRESSION!

"Use a SUCCESS INSPIRATION instead of a MOTIVATION one (my emphasis)." Actually the Ducketts say this goes against most of what you have heard. The Ducketts say: "Motivation moves you AWAY from something you don't want and INSPIRATION moves you TOWARDS something you do want (my emphasis)."

Let's use a skill for Preparedness and Survival as an example. You don't want to find yourself out on the Appalachian Trail, where we run our western North Carolina boot camp, with a broken arm and not knowing how to make a splint. So using the visualizing we spoke about and the Fear Run Down exercise, you realize that learning everything you can about Wilderness First Aid is INSPIRATION for taking a course. You want to be **Prepared Not Scared!**

Another book that is a MUST is *Extreme Ownership* (again Resources at my SituationalAwareness.Expert (http://www.situationalawareness.expert) by two former US Navy SEALs commanding forces at Ramadi in Iraq, which was the most violent urban warfare ever encountered by SEALs!

Extreme Ownership refers to YOU being ultimately RESPONSIBLE for the mission! You can't play the BLAME game! WHINING AND COMPLAINING NOT ALLOWED!

So is F.E.A.R. located in your brain? Absolutely! Remember the book *Deep Survival* (Resources on my website) mentioned before? Here is what it says:

"During a fear reaction, the AMYGDALA (as with most structures in the brain, there are two of them, one in each hemisphere), in concert with numerous other structures in the brain and body help to trigger a staggeringly complex sequence of events, all aimed at producing a behavior to promote SURVIVAL (my emphasis) freezing in place, for example, followed by running away."

Yes you most likely have heard of the flee or fight syndrome. This is related to the AMYGDALA.

The author Gonzales says that actually the AMYGDALA can get you in trouble! He says: "Even as the hormones produced under STRESS (my emphasis) disrupt perception, thinking, and the formation and retrieval of memories, they set a potentially dangerous TRAP (my emphasis) by exciting the amygdala. They help to dampen explicit (conscious) MEMORY (my emphasis) even while creating and recalling implicit (unconscious) memories with greater efficiency. As the fear rises, you become more unable to deal with it because you're not even AWARE (my emphasis) of the learning that's propelling you."

So how can you avoid the AMYGDALA taking control? This might surprise you – LAUGHTER AND HUMOR! Gonzales says: "There is evidence that LAUGHTER (my emphasis) can send chemical signals to actively INHIBIT (my emphasis) the firing of nerves in the amygdala, thereby DAMPENING FEAR (my emphasis)."

Here is another thing I have learned recently from the late BILLIONAIRE BILL BARTMANN in his excellent book entitled *Billionaire Secrets to Success* (see Resources at SituationalAwareness.Expert (http://www.situationalawareness.expert).

Bill talks about SELF BELIEF and how the brain can help you.

"Self-belief (or self-esteem) is the internal image our subconscious mind has of itself as it relates to how we feel about our personal capabilities to accomplish certain tasks...It doesn't matter that the image of self as held by our subconscious mind may be INACCURATE (my emphasis), or that it may (or may not) be CONSISTENT (my emphasis) with the view others have of us as individuals."

"Self-belief is deeply rooted in the mind because it is tightly connected to our inherent SURVIVAL INSTINCT- SELF PRESERVATION (my emphasis)."

"Our self-preservation instinct has only one mission – to PROTECT AND PRESERVE (my emphasis) the life support system within which it is housed – our mental and physical being."

"Our self-preservation will not, I will repeat WILL NOT, let us do anything it perceives as HARMFUL (my emphasis)..."

Of course we have learned that due to PREVIOUS information about EMOTIONAL MARKERS, MENTAL MAPS and the AMYGDALA all about SELF-PRESERVATION can go south!!

Bill shared another thing I had NEVER seen in my previous reading of literally hundreds of these type books that makes TOTAL sense!

We all know about SETTING GOALS; however are you aware from your own experience that many times these goals are NOT reached? I certainly am!

I have set hundreds of them and I bet only a dozen have been accomplished!

Why is this the situations?

Bill says in his book that the MIND is ALWAYS wanting to make sure you are not EMBARRASSED OR HARMED! So in the past the mind knew that I might not be able to bring the goal about and I would feel EMBARRASSMENT and even PAIN!

Well here is how Bill says you can get those dreams, missions and visions to REALITY!

Instead of setting GOALS you make PROMISES!

Yes PROMISES! Bill says research has found that once you make a PROMISE to yourself, family, relatives, friends or God, you are way more likely to achieve the PROMISE!

Why?

Well he shares the following:

Emotional Attachment: "A promise carries with it a much deeper sense of RESPONSIBILITY (my emphasis) to the person to whom it is made, whether that person is you or someone else…When you make a promise, your emotions are INVOLVED (my emphasis)…We do NOT (my emphasis) make promises we do not INTEND TO KEEP (my emphasis)."

History of Success: "Our mind recognizes that we have a history of SUCCESS (my emphasis) when it comes to making promises…Rather than being preconditioned for failure (because of a history of failure), our mind is PRECONDITIONED FOR SUCCESS (my emphasis)."

Role Reversal of Our Subconscious Mind: "If you fail to keep a promise made, you will suffer (experience) an emotional reaction: SHAME, EMBARRASSMENT, OR DISAPPOINTMENT (my emphasis). Remember, our subconscious mind does NOT (my emphasis) want us to fail or suffer the emotional pain of EMBARRASSMENT OR HUMILIATION (my emphasis). So what does it do? It helps us keep our promise (self-survival)."

So at the end of the book I am going to share my long time PROMISE to God, myself and business partners. In the mean time think of a PROMISE OR PROMISES you would like to make!

NOTES:

CHAPTER 4
Preparedness

Preparing for a disaster is not as daunting as it may seem at first glance, as long as you are willing to listen, learn and put in the work to make yourself ready. Like other areas of life, planning for an emergency isn't a one-time event; rather, it should be an ongoing process. Emergencies come in many forms – accidents, fires, tornadoes, floods or a whole swarm of unexpected events – and being prepared means being able to recover with a minimum of aggravation. A disaster, on the other hand, requires more complete planning if you are to recover with your family and assets intact.

Being prepared for a disaster requires understanding the four phases of emergency preparedness, and what to do during each phase. **The first phase is being prepared for emergencies.** That means identifying and understanding the kinds of disasters that could happen where you live so that you can plan appropriately. You don't have to worry about hurricanes if you live in North Dakota, but you do have to prepare for floods, blizzards, tornadoes, or a host of other problems. The most important aspect of preparation is to have a plan, have a disaster kit, and practice what you will do during a variety of situations.

Sometimes you will need to shelter in place, and have a minimum of 3 days worth of food and water at home – at least that is what the government recommends. We recommend at least 6 MONTHS worth of supplies, since you never know how quickly your community can recover from an incident – if it can recover at all. You may also be asked – or decide on your own – to quickly evacuate from your home. Your BUG-OUT BACKPACK (www.battlelakeoutdoors.com) will be different from your "shelter at home" kit and should include the Lawson Hammock/Tent (www.lawsonhammock.com) for each member of your family that can be easily carried in either your backpack or SLACK PACK (www.battlelakeoutdoors.com) for kids under 10 in your family.

The second phase of being prepared is the response phase. In a disaster, by definition you are the first responder to the scene – you are already there. It may be a while, up to days, before fire, rescue or police can come to your aid. Your survival and recovery are really up to you. The better prepared you are, the better your response will be, and the quicker you, your family and your community will recover. At the very least, you should take a first aid class, and understand basic rescue techniques. Remember Hurricane Harvey? Those that fared best were those that were prepared to respond, and/or had the means to leave the area. If you live in a flood-prone hurricane zone, you should be prepared ... it's not like you don't know what can happen. The greater the potential for catastrophe, the more you need to prepare. And since you never know when a calamity will strike, prepare for the worst!

The third phase of being prepared is the recovery phase. This is when you work towards getting back to "normal". Chances are there will be a lot of work to do – repairing property, cleaning up, maybe even completely rebuilding. But there may be emotional clean up as well.

The final phase of emergency preparedness is hazard mitigation. This means looking around you and seeing what you can do before an emergency to lessen the impact, and after an emergency, reevaluating what you did to see if there were things that you could do better next time. It can mean simple things like bringing in your lawn furniture before the storm hits, or boarding up your windows before the hurricane. It can mean having a "winter kit" in your car with food, water, candles and blankets. Or it can mean getting together with your neighbors and forming a neighborhood watch. The fact that you are reading this book shows that you have taken the initial step in mitigating a coming disaster.

First and foremost, pay attention to what is going on around you – not just in your neighborhood, but meteorologically and politically. The mainstream media may not tell you what you need to know – you have to proactively search across multiple sources to get an understanding of what is coming. Pay attention. Watching your local news or The Weather Channel may help you prepare for weather-related events, but your local news may not warn you about political unrest or if a pandemic is brewing across the world.

Your first mission is to help form a neighborhood group just like you would do for fun get- togethers. If you do not know your neighbors, now is the time to go door to door and invite them to a meeting at your home or the club house at a condo or apartment complex.

This would be an excellent time for you to suggest that the group form a food cooperative or start a community garden. In some areas - even in urban areas - there is what are called CSAs – Community Service Agriculture operations. This is where the owner offers shares in his operation/farm and you buy a share that usually ranges from $500-1000 per share. This gives him the upfront money to develop the farm hopefully in an organic style. Then when the harvest comes in you get an equal share throughout the year. If you don't want to put up with the hassle of gardening then your group could look into purchasing a Bioponica unit from me. Just send me an email at mrvalentineknightstemplar@gmail.com with Subject: Bioponica. Here is a video I did with co-inventor Dr David - https://youtu.be/NAKYbolbYjg.

You and your family should start storing food and water immediately. When you go to the grocery store, buy double the amount of canned goods and packaged goods each week until you have at least a 3-6 months supply on hand. Canned and packaged goods are not as healthy for you as fresh or even frozen foods but when you are in a survival mode you eat what is available! You should also consider buying as a group from a dehydrated/freeze dried food merchant like Wise or Food4Patriots. Both are very tasty!

Acquire an Adequate Water Supply

1. First, determine how much water you and your family will need. It will be used for drinking, cooking, washing your hands, brushing your teeth, etc. The average person is going to need at least one gallon per day.

2. The majority of the tap water available during a disaster like the recent 2017 hurricanes may not be safe to drink. Therefore you should look for an alternative source of drinking water. For instance, if you are having it delivered to your home; you might consider having them deliver double the usual amount. You would then take the excess water and transfer it into FDA-approved water storage containers. These storage containers then should be placed on their sides and stacked up. You can find these at your local Walmart or Kmart.

3. You might want to see if your local grocery store has water vending machines. Many stores offer this service to their patrons at minimal cost. The water is processed using reverse osmosis, which produces some of the best water you can get. Do not use discarded plastic milk jugs or fruit juice containers to store drinking water! Milk proteins and fruit sugars can remain in the container and can fuel bacterial growth when water is stored in them. Conserve your stored water!

4. Use tap water as long as it is available, but with the unreliability of the local water system during an emergency situation, be sure to allow any tap water to boil for at least 10 minutes before you drink it.

5. Another consideration is using either chlorine bleach or iodine for decontaminating your drinking water. Disinfecting with household bleach kills many

– but not all – disease-causing organisms. When you buy the chlorine bleach you must make sure the label states that it contains at least 5.5% sodium chloride. Bargain brands are usually not good enough for this use. You will use 8 drops per gallon for most decontamination and you should be able to both taste and smell the chloride in the water. Also if the water is cloudy, immediately add 16 drops per gallon in the beginning. Then you should mix thoroughly and allow the water to stand for at least 30 minutes before drinking. You should still notice a slight smell and taste of chlorine. If not, then repeat the above steps. You can mask the taste and odor with a powdered drink mix, if you want. Iodine is not as effective as chlorine in controlling the parasite Giardia, but it's better than no treatment at all. Remember, though, that iodine should not be used by people with thyroid problems.

6. There are going to be times when you will need emergency water, which you should definitely decontaminate before using. First, you can use the water in the toilet tank (not the bowl), but only if you have never used a "toilet bowl sanitizer" – the kind that hangs in the tank. Second, you can use the water from your hot water heater. You can attach a garden hose at the bottom of the hot water heater. Be sure you have turned off the heat before using the procedure and also drain out sediment that collects in the bottom of the heater.

7. When you are storing your processed water, be sure to keep the containers away from strong odors and off the ground or concrete floors. You will want to rotate the water containers as you purify and store the additional supplies, using the older water first.

8. You are going to need some sources of non-drinking water for bathing, washing clothes, flushing toilets, etc. You can use your old plastic milk containers for the non-drinking water storage. Good sources are rainwater, rivers, lakes, streams and brooks. You can collect rainwater in containers placed underneath the spouts on the roof gutters. Many county extension offices around the country hold workshops on building rain barrels.

Your best bet is to purchase immediately some of those 55 gallon water containers that meet Federal standards. Remember you should have ONE GALLON of fresh water for every member of the family for every day. So if you are a family of four and disaster strikes, then you are going to need water for not weeks but possibly months. So we will say there are 31 days X 4 members X 6 months. That comes to 704 gallons. If the problem is not resolved in six months then you might have to have a full year supply or 1408 gallons. So how many 55-gallon containers are you going to need? For 6 months you will need 13 containers or 26 for a year.

Obtaining Emergency & Survival Food

It is necessary to have a food supply with a long-term shelf life. There are many companies that prepare such food through dehydration and create packaging that will maintain the nutritional integrity of the food for several years. If you Google "emergency and survival food" you should find one that will meet your needs like Wise and Food4Patriots.

Regular canned goods have a longer shelf life than you might imagine. Look on the can for the product code and an 800 number. The person who answers the phone will ask you for the code. They will then be able to tell you when this can was sealed and the average shelf- life of the can. Surprisingly, most of the canned goods have a shelf life of at least 2-5 years!

When you are buying your canned goods, consider buying in the very large economy sizes, especially if you are a neighborhood group. You can even find these sizes at grocery stores, Sam's Club and Costco. If you have the "in" to a food supply company for restaurants then you can find some really great sizes and good, low prices.

White rice is another staple you need to stock up on. Why white rice instead of brown rice? It lasts longer! Dried beans will store almost indefinitely in an airtight container. Combining rice and beans in a meal creates a complete protein chain for your body – important when meat proteins are in short supply. Also, you will want to collect up an assortment of grains. Always store the rice and grains in FDA-approved containers. Before you store them, place them in large food storage bags. Now replace the container lid and seal it with duct tape. Also place the container on its side so the contents can be accessed without having to re-stack your entire shelf.

Again you could grow all your veggies and fruit yourself or with your neighbors but I will tell it can quickly become a chore. Also insects can wreak havoc on your garden.

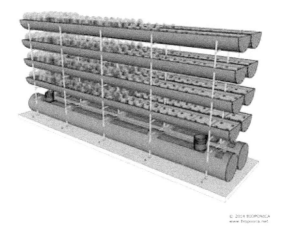

That is why I strongly recommend you look into some form of HYDROPONICS or Bioponica that I work with. The Bioponica unit also means you don't have to develop the structure for it and maintain it constantly. With Bioponica you can maintain it for only an hour per day at the most! Again email me at mrvalentineknightstemplar@gmail.com   Subject: Bioponica.

Essentials

So here is an **essential** list of products and services you will need. We strongly suggest you start setting aside funds **now** for the necessities you and your family will need. Do not wait because a number of these necessities are going to be expensive and supplies could become limited. For instance, if you are looking at dehydrated and or freeze-dried foods you may be hard pressed to find them as the US military is reportedly stockpiling them.

1. Minimum of 1 year of dehydrated/freeze-dried food for each family member.
2. Minimum of 1 year of vitamins and minerals and other supplements for each family member.
3. Minimum of 1 year of first aid items for each family member (that would be in addition to the EMT kit for the community).
4. Minimum of 1 year of prescription and over-the-counter drug items for each for each member.
5. Minimum of 1 year of **non-hybrid** seeds for a garden. If you are establishing a community, you might have each family decide which type of seeds they would like to contribute to the garden.

6. Minimum of 1 year of clothing for **all seasons** for each member of the family.

7. A 4-season tent large enough to accommodate every member of the family. Also well insulated sleeping bags. Some of you could get by with a 3-season tent in the more temperate zones like my 200 square foot one from Kmart.

8. Fishing and hunting gear.

9. Assortment of sturdy gardening tools and yard tools.

10. Comprehensive and sturdy tool kit that can be used for construction and vehicle repair.

11. **Non-electric** water purification system.

12. **Non-electric** dehydrator.

13. **Non-electronic** compact fitness system and sports equipment for playing games such as football, baseball, basketball, badminton, volleyball, soccer, darts, shuffleboard, ping pong, etc.

14. Buy **high-quality** 2-way radios with a minimum 2 year supply of rechargeable batteries for each member of the family. They should last 100-200 recharges. Consider also becoming a ham radio operator like am I doing.

15. Fire-proof valuable box.

16. Assortment of photos and memorabilia for each family member to connect with the past and share his/her story with other community members.

17. **Large** supply of ingredients for making safe, non-toxic, personal home care products and medicinal tinctures.

Of course, these are ESSENTIALS and you will notice I mentioned NO weapons. I personally have several handguns, a rifle, a shotgun and even a high powered crossbow, which was of course used by the Knights Templars. If you do not want to have these type of weapons, I still recommend you have several knives of different sizes.

NOTES:

CHAPTER 5

Canning

My friend Bernice was shopping in western North Carolina when she saw an older lady buying dozens of CANNING JARS. Bernice asked the old lady why she was buying so many. The old lady looked at Bernice and without batting an eye told her:

"Child, if you don't know how to can vegetables and fruits then you better get cracking. We older folks here in these mountains have a bad feeling that something is going to be happening soon and those that have not laid up there stores will be a-hurtin. And, child, this not near enough jars for you and your family."

This old woman, who had lived through the Great Depression, foresaw what could happen again!

When Bernice shared this story with me, I KNEW that I had to find out more about canning and tell you about how to can your vegetables and fruits that you will be growing in your garden or hydroponically. So here is a fairly in depth how-to.

First, you have to have the right canner for each type of product. For instance, with foods that have a high acid content (pH of 4.6 and lower) such as fruits and pickled vegetables you can use a boiling-water-bath canner. You can process these acid foods safely in boiling water. For all common vegetables, including tomatoes, you need to use a steam-pressure canner. By the way, contrary to what people say tomatoes are NOT vegetables – they are fruits -

but the modern varieties have a lower acid content than older, or heritage, varieties. You will need to add a little bit of acid, usually in the form of lemon juice, to your tomatoes to make them safe to can. Some people still use a water-bath canner for their tomatoes, but modern agricultural extensions now recommend steam-pressure canning.

Let's talk about the steam-pressure canner first. For safe operation of your canner, follow the manufacturers directions carefully. Clean petcock and safety-valve openings by drawing a string or narrow strip of cloth through them. Do this at the beginning of the canning season and often during the season. Check the pressure gauge An accurate pressure gauge is necessary to get the processing temperatures needed to make food keep. The weighted gauge needs to be thoroughly clean. A dial gauge, old or new, should be checked before the canning season, and also during the season, if you use the canner often. Your county extension office will usually test your gauge for free.

If your gauge is off 5 pounds or more, you'd better get a new one. But if the gauge is not off more than 4 pounds, you can correct it as shown below. As a reminder, tie on the canner a tag stating the reading to use to get the correct pressure.

The food is to be processed at 10 pounds steam pressure; so

If the gauge reads **high**,

- ❖ 1 pound high…process at 11 pounds
- ❖ 2 pounds high…process at 12 pounds

- ❖ 3 pounds high…process at 13 pounds
- ❖ 4 pounds high…process at 14 pounds

If the gauge reads **low**,

- ❖ 1 pound low…process at 9 pounds
- ❖ 2 pounds low…process at 8 pounds
- ❖ 3 pounds low…process at 7 pounds
- ❖ 4 pounds low…process at 6 pounds

Make sure and thoroughly clean your canner. Wash canner kettle well if you have not used it in a long time. Dry well.

Next we have the water-bath canner. Any big metal container may be used as a boiling water-bath canner if it is deep enough so that the water is well over the tops of the jars and has space to boil freely. Allow 2 to 4 inches above jar tops for brisk boiling. The canner must have a tight fitting cover and wire or wooden rack. If the rack has dividers, jars will not touch each other or fall against the sides of the canner during processing. If a steam-pressure canner is deep enough, you can use it for a water bath. Cover, but do NOT fasten. Leave petcock wide open, so the steam escapes and pressure does not build up inside the canner.

Glass Jars

Glass home canning jars, sometimes called Mason Jars, are the ONLY ones recommended for home canning. They are made specifically so that the canning lid will form an airtight seal as part of the canning process. Before use, be sure all jars and closures are perfect. **Discard any with cracks, chips, dents or rust; defects prevent airtight seals.** Jars can be re-used safely for many years, but they will eventually wear out or become damaged.

The lids come in two parts, lids and bands and come in regular and wide mouth varieties. The lid has a flanged edge that is coated with a sealing compound on one side. Select the size of closure – wide mouth or regular – that fits your jars. Use new lids EVERY time; they are not reusable. The bands can be reused if they are still in good condition. Wash glass jars in hot, soapy water and they might need boiling or holding in boiling water for a few minutes. Make sure and follow the manufacturer's directions. Glass jars that seal with a jar rubber should NOT be used for canning, as you cannot test to see if the closure is really sealed.

One of my email list members shared this with me before we went to press: "Do you know that you can use any jar with a fitting metal lid which has a rubber seal in the lid such as glass jars bought from the supermarket; pasta sauce jars and bottles and other glass containers for pickles, mustard, mayonnaise, sauerkraut, etc.? These jars can be be reused for a number of years and cost nothing!" THANKS Meta for this helpful insight from a professional canner!

In recent years a new product has come on the market that provides reusable canning lids. They aren't common, but the product may save money in the long run.

Tin Cans

Using tin cans instead of glass jars is another home canning method. They are not commonly available, and you need specialized equipment for this method, but they do have the added advantage of being lighter in weight and less prone to breakage. Good to know if you need to grab your home canned food and bug out during a disaster!

Three types of tin cans are used in home canning – plain tin, C-enamel and R-enamel. For most products plain tin cans are satisfactory. Enameled cans are recommended for certain fruits and vegetables to prevent discoloration of food, but they are not necessary for a wholesome product.

C-enamel is recommended for corn and hominy. R-enamel is recommended for beets, red berries, red or black cherries, plums, pumpkin, rhubarb and winter squash. Plain tin cans are recommended for all other fruits and vegetables.

Most all of the fruits and vegetables are canned in Number 2 and 2 1/2 tin cans. A Number 2 can hold about 2 1/2 cups and a Number 2 1/2 can about 3 1/2 cups.

Use cans only in GOOD condition! See that cans, lids and gaskets are perfect. **Discard badly bent, dented, or rusted cans, and lids with damaged gaskets.** Keep lids in paper packing until ready to use. The paper protects the lids from dirt and moisture.

Just before use, wash cans in clean water; drain upside down. Do NOT wash lids as washing may damage the gaskets. If lids are dusty or dirty, rinse with clean water or wipe with a damp cloth just before you put them on the cans.

Make sure and check the sealer! Make sure the sealer you use is properly adjusted. To test, put a little water into a can, seal it, and then submerge can in boiling water for a few seconds. If air bubbles rise from around the can, the seam is not tight. Adjust sealer following the manufacturer's directions.

General Canning Procedure

Choose fresh, firm fruits and young tender vegetables. For the best quality in the canned product, use only perfect fruits and vegetables. Eat the ones now that you aren't going to can! Sort them for size and ripeness; they cook more evenly that way.

Filling Containers

Fruits and vegetables may be packed raw into glass jars and tin cans or preheated and packed hot. Most raw fruits and vegetables should be packed tightly into the container because they will shrink during processing. A few vegetables like corn, lima beans and peas should be packed loosely because they expand.

Hot food should be packed fairly loosely. It should be at or near boiling temperature when it is packed.

There should be enough syrup, water or juice to fill in around the solid food in the container and to cover the food. Food at the top of the container tends to darken if not covered with liquid. It takes from 1/2 to 1 1/2 cups of liquid for a quart glass jar or a

Number 2 1/2 tin can. With only a few exceptions, some space should be left between the packed food and the closure. Canning recipes will specifically state the "head space" – the gap between food/liquid and the top of the jar – for the specific food you are canning. As a general rule, leave 1 inch of head space for low-acid foods, vegetables and meats, 1/2 inch head space for juices, jams, jellies and pickles.

Closing Glass Jars

Wash both lids and bands in hot, soapy water, but don't use any abrasive materials or cleansers that might scratch or damage the coating. Rinse in hot water. Bands may be dried before use, but the lids must be heated for 10 minutes to help achieve a good vacuum seal. Place lids in water to cover and simmer for 10 minutes, or until ready to use. Wipe the top of your filled jar with a clean, damp cloth and place the lid on the jar rim. Place a band over the lid and screw it onto the jar just until fingertip tight.

Exhausting and Sealing Tin Cans

Tin cans are sealed before processing. The temperature of the food in the cans must be 170 degrees F or higher when cans are sealed. Food is heated to this temperature to drive out air so that there will be a good vacuum in the can after processing and cooling. Removal of the air also helps prevent discoloring of canned food and change in flavor.

Food packed raw must be heated in the cans (exhausted) before the cans are sealed. Food packed hot may be sealed without further heating if you are sure the temperature of the food has not dropped below 170 degrees F. To make sure, test with a thermometer placing the bulb at the center of the can. If the thermometer registers lower than 170 degrees F or if you do not make the test, exhaust the cans.

To exhaust, place open, filled cans on a rack in a kettle in which there is enough boiling water to come to about 2 inches below the tops of the cans. Cover the kettle and bring water back to boiling. Boil until a thermometer inserted at the center of the can registers 170 degrees F or for the length of time given in the directions for the fruit or vegetable you are canning.

Remove the cans from the water one at a time, and add boiling packing liquid or water if necessary to bring head space back to the level specified for each product. Place clean lid on filled can. Seal at once!

Cooling Canned Food

Carefully remove the glass jars from the canner with a jar lifter. If liquid boiled out in processing, do NOT open jar to add more! Cool jars topside up. Give each jar enough room to let air get at all sides. Never set a jar on a cold surface; instead set the jars on a rack or on a folded cloth. Keep hot jars away from drafts, but don't slow cooling by covering them. You will probably hear the jars "pop" as the vacuum seals the lid during the cooling process.

With tin cans, put them in cold, clean water to cool them; change water as needed to cools cans quickly. Take cans out of the water while they are still warm so they will dry in the air. If you stack cans stagger them so that the air can get around them.

Day-After Canning Jobs

Test the seal on glass jars with porcelain-lined caps by turning each jar partly over in your hands. To test a jar that has a flat metal lid, press center of the lid. If the lid is down and will not move, the jar is sealed. Or tap the center of the lid with a spoon. A clear, ringing sound means a good seal. A dull note does not always mean a poor seal. Store jars without leaks and check for spoilage before using them.

If you find a leaky jar, use unspoiled food right away or can it again. Before using the jar or lid check for defects.

Before storing canned food, wipe containers clean. Label to show contents, date and lot number.

Storing Canned Food

Properly canned food stored in a cool, dry place will retain good eating quality for a year. Storing canned food in a warm place near hot pipes, a range or a furnace, or direct sunlight may is NOT a good idea. Dampness may corrode cans or metal lids and cause leakage so the food will spoil.

Freezing does not cause food spoilage unless the seal is damaged or the jar is broken. However, frozen canned food may be less palatable than properly stored canned food. In an unheated storage place it is well advised to protect canned food by wrapping the jars in paper or covering them with a blanket.

On Guard Against Spoilage

Don't use canned food that shows any sign of spoilage. Look closely at each container before opening it. **Bulging can ends, jar lids, rings, or a leak may indicate that the seal has broken and the food has spoiled!** When you open a container look for other signs like spurting liquid, an off odor or mold. **When in doubt, throw it out.**

It's possible for canned vegetables to contain the poison causing botulism, which is a VERY serious food poisoning, without showing signs of spoilage. To avoid any risk of botulism, it is essential that the pressure canner be in perfect order and that every canning recommendation be followed exactly! Unless you are ABSOLUTELY sure of the gauge and canning methods, BOIL home-canned vegetables before tasting. Heating usually makes any odor of spoilage more noticeable.

Bring vegetables to a ROLLING boil; then cover and boil for at least 10 minutes. Boil spinach and corn 20 minutes. If the food looks spoiled, foams, or has an off odor during heating, **DESTROY IT!**

BURN spoiled vegetables or DISPOSE of the food so that it will not be eaten by humans or animals! It is imperative that you follow the above to the letter to avoid potentially DEADLY botulism!

Processing in Boiling-Water Bath

Put filled glass jars or tin cans into canner containing HOT or BOILING water. Add boiling water if needed to bring water an inch or two over tops of the containers; don't pour boiling water directly on glass jars! Put cover on canner. When water in canner comes to a rolling boil, start to count processing time. Boil gently and steadily for the time recommended for the food you are canning. Add boiling water during processing if needed to keep containers covered. Remove containers from the canner when processing time is up. Here are the times according to the altitude at which you live:

Increase in processing time if the time called for is:

Altitude at 20 minutes or less
- 1,000 feet – 1 minute
- 2,000 feet – 2 minutes
- 3,000 feet – 3 minutes
- 4,000 feet – 4 minutes
- 5,000 feet – 5 minutes
- 6,000 feet – 6 minutes
- 7,000 feet – 7 minutes
- 8,000 feet – 8 minutes
- 9,000 feet – 9 minutes
- 10,000 feet – 10 minutes

If it is over 20 minutes, DOUBLE the amount of minutes for each of the 1000 feet INCREASE i.e. 1000 feet – 2 minutes, 2000 feet – 4 minutes

To Figure Yield of Canned Fruit from Fresh

The number of quarts of canned food you can get from a given quantity of fresh fruit depends upon the quality, variety, maturity and size of the fruit and whether it is whole, in halves or in slices and also whether it is packed raw or hot. You will need the suggested amount of fruit or tomatoes in pounds to make 1 quart of canned food:

- Apples – 2 1/2 - 3 lbs.
- Berries (except strawberries) – 1 1/2 - 3 lbs.
- Cherries (canned pitted) – 2 – 2 1/2 lbs.
- Peaches – 2 – 3 lbs.
- Pears – 2 -3 lbs.
- Plums – 1 1/2 - 2 1/2 lbs.
- Tomatoes – 2 1/2 - 3 1/2 lbs. (YES they are fruits!)

For processing times for vegetables you need to again be aware of your altitude. For instance if you live at 2000 feet or less above sea level, process vegetables at 10 pounds pressure for the times given. At 2000 feet you should process at 11 pounds pressure, at 4000 feet at 12 pounds, at 6000 feet at 13 pounds, at 8000 feet at 14 pounds, and at 10,000 feet at 15 pounds pressure.

Below are the yields for a quart from the amount of pounds needed:

- Asparagus…2 1/2 lbs.
- Beans, lima, in pods…3 to 5 lbs.
- Beans, snap…1 1/2 to 2 1/2 lbs.
- Beets, without tops…2 to 3 1/2 lbs.

- Carrots, without tops…2 to 3 lbs.
- Corn, sweet in husks…3 to 6 lbs.
- Okra…1 1⁄2 lbs.
- Peas, green, in pods…3 to 6 lbs.
- Pumpkin or winter squash…1 1⁄2 to 3 lbs.
- Spinach and other greens…2 to 6 lbs.
- Squash, summer…2 to 4 lbs.
- Sweet potatoes…2 to 3 lbs.

This should be enough to get you going. There are many good books available on canning – be sure to have one or two in your library. Your county extension office will often have classes or free literature available. Canning jars and supplies are readily available everywhere from grocery and hardware stores to multiple online specialty outfits.

NOTES:

CHAPTER 6
Off-The-Grid

You would be wise to also consider "off-the-grid" sources of power. So what are your choices for alternative sources of electric power?

From Nature, you can use the sun, the wind, and flowing water. Or, you can use candles, kerosene lamps, and batteries. You will need power for lighting, cooking, heating and communication systems. You must have power to run appliances and electronics. You can begin by stocking up on candles, especially the 7-day variety and those with multiple wicks. More illumination can be obtained from kerosene lamps or camping lanterns that use Coleman fuel and unleaded gas. Also there are propane lanterns that allow you to adjust the amount of light generated to as much as 400 watts. Another newer source is the long lasting LED lamps, lanterns, flashlights, etc.

More power means the consumption of more fuel at a faster rate. A generator rated at 8000 watts or higher is ideal in most situations; a 5000 watt generator will cover your basic service; and a 3000 watt generator will probably provide sufficient basic lighting and also power a few small appliances.

You must also consider batteries. We are not referring to the energizers from the Pink Bunny or even batteries used in vehicles, but to 12-volt, deep cycle, marine batteries that will provide at least 100 hours of service. You can also generate a great deal of AC current that will stay charged using only one small solar panel placed on the ground. You can actually hook up as many of these 12-volt marine batteries as you desire, creating even more power "off the grid." For information on using these batteries, Google "marine battery power."

If you are looking at going solar, then you need to make sure that you know what you are doing! For instance, don't try to place your photovoltaic (PV) system on the roof. An expert told me that seldom are these systems placed on roofs because of "wind loading," which occurs when a high wind gets under the PV installation and creates a "kite flying" situation! Another reason you should avoid roof insulation is the potential of poking holes and causing leaks. You would want to consider placing the system on the ground or on poles.

I am sure many of you would like solar panels or this new system but don't have the budget for them. The late Sun Bear, a Native American shaman, shares here how to make a very inexpensive one:

"Take a piece of corrugated tin roofing material smaller than 4 feet by 8 feet and build a shallow box to hold it – 4 inches deep and 8 feet long by 4 feet wide (a piece of plywood works as well as a back for this box). Name one of the 4'X4" sides the bottom end and the other the top end. There must be screened vents in the bottom and top ends. The area of these openings should be in a ratio of 3 (bottom) to 6 (top). Paint the inside of the box flat black along with the roofing material and nail it into the box. Cover the entire box with a piece of glass and seal it with silicon sealant. The solar panel works best if it facing due south and is at an angle that is perpendicular to the noonday sun."

Also do a Google search for "do-it-yourself" solar panels.

What you see here is what is called a Crank-A-Watt ™ invented by my good friend Tim Moeller of Moeller Engineering. Also Tim has authorized a friend of mine Steve to manufacture it. Using Nicolas Tesla (Google him!) technology this hand cranked 400 watt generator uses only a small lawn mower battery! Again I can help you get these generators from either Tim or Steve at a good price by sending me an email at mrvalentineknightstemplar@gmail.com Subject: Crank-A-Watt ™

NOTES:

CHAPTER 7

Tent Living

As I may have mentioned I actual spent over 6 MONTHS living in this TENT at 68 years young just to see if I could do it. Here is a video: Tent Living - https://youtu.be/8IGwkUZN8Wo.

I used a 200 square foot K-mart tent that even though it was made for only three seasons made it through ice and snow! Of course I had to keep brushing it off.

200 square feet was plenty room for a single guy! I had my sleeping bag, a blowup chair and ottoman, a three drawer chest, my desk, another four level shelf unit, an enclosed clothing rack, and numerous snap top containers of every size. Outside I had a

CleanWaste (http://www.cleanwaste.com) portable toilet enclosed in its own tent that is used by the US military. Also I had Lodge (http://www.lodgemfg.com) tripod that held my Lodge Dutch oven. I had a mini-barbecue unit and a Global Sun Oven (http://www.sunoven.com). Finally I had one of those solar showers for bathing either inside the CleanWaste tent or outside on a warm day.

I was the LEAST stressed out I had been in years!

I would wake up in the morning to birds right above my tent.

Another item that I had in the tent was the previously discussed Crank-A-Watt ™. It is Made in the USA and can be BIKE powered! It is also NOT one of those cheap small hand held units that sell for around $60. Those cheap small units are limited to charging cell phones, net portables and tablets.

I was amazed to see that there are still Made in the USA plastic compartmental plates, cups and cutlery which I found at OpenCountry (http://www.opencountrycampware.com) . They even make a 12 cup coffee percolator that will come in handy in your camping adventures. You can actually get everything you need if you purchase their 6 Person Non-stick Camp Set.

My friend John, who owns Battle Lake Outdoors (http://www.battlelakeoutdoors.com), who supplies me with both my USA Made backpack and slack pack also sent me his Deluxe Cargo Duffle Bag which measures 36" x 16" where I can get almost everything I need in it for my Tent Living.

Speaking of backpacks you NEVER want to get one of those flimsy foreign made ones from Walmart or Kmart. They have a tendency to have the straps rip away from the backpack even with 35 pounds. Battle Lake Outdoors backpacks can handle up to 50 pounds or possibly more! The last thing you want when you are Bugging Out is to have a strap break!

I sure hope you have a backpack for every member of the family 10 years old or older and a slack pack for the younger members. Each member needs the Lawson Hammock/Tent (http://www.lawsonhammock.com) combination with tree huggers; three days of water and food that my good friends at Survivor Industries (http://www.survivorind.com) supply me; a sleeping bag and a change of clothes along with toiletries. One of the adults needs to carry the Sawyer (http://www.sawyer.com)Water Filtration unit that cleans 100,000 GALLONS of water, the Sawyer (http://www.sawyer.com) Sting & Bite kit, a military quality first aid kit, a portable shortwave radio, possibly a portable ham radio like I will be carrying, a compass, a mess kit like the one from OpenCountry, break-open flares, the Zaps Gear (http://www.zapsgear.com) Survival Grenade, etc.

HERE (https://youtu.be/L-UJUtHm2ks) is a video I did with my Bug-Out backpack for a documentary team from Denmark.

NOTES:

CHAPTER 8
Two-Wheel Bugging-Out!

In the past I have told my clients they have to be FIT enough to walk comfortably up to 20 MILES DAILY! As we know your SAFE AREA should be a MINIMUM of 100 MILES from an urban area like Atlanta.

Many said that especially with small children this would be next to impossible. So that is when I came up with TWO-WHEEL BUGGING OUT which I wrote about in *SurvivorsEdge*.

Of course I tell them you want to have a QUALITY STURDY MOUNTAIN BIKE for EACH person. Of course there may be babies to contend with and that is when you have to have one of those Allen Sports (http://www.allensportsusa.com) strollers that can be attached to a bike. One member can handle this and another one can pull the Sports Explorer Cargo

Trailer from Allen Sports like the one I use on my Mongoose (http://www.mongoose.com) Torment. This trailer can hold easily up to 75 pounds and is totally enclosed.

Here are some important points I shared in the article:

- ❖ If you buy preassembled, make sure you check EVERY bolt, screw, and nut is on TIGHT! If in doubt, find a QUALIFIED service rep to check it out before riding.
- ❖ Even if preassembled, read EVERY page of the manual so you know how to repair any problem without looking at the manual while on the road!
- ❖ Keep RUST from your bike!
- ❖ Do a MONTHLY check to make sure it is in TOP riding condition!
- ❖ Have EXTRA tubes, bolts, nuts, screws, etc. along with a tool kit for your particular bike!

Remember your mountain bike and the cargo trailer and or stroller are INVESTMENTS!

NOTES:

CHAPTER 9
Safe Area & Eco-Villages

Okay you have heard me talk about getting to your SAFE AREA. If you remember this should be at least 100 MILES from an urban area like Atlanta. I'm actually 123 miles from Atlanta!

With the use of bikes as I discussed in the last chapter you should be able to average 20 miles daily. Of course with children this could be considerably less.

So how do you find a SAFE AREA?

I would take a map and draw a circle with a compass (no not the one you use to find where you are going!) measuring 100 miles from the location of your home. Then I would begin Googling each area that has a small town like my Franklin, NC.

Since you may be in your SAFE AREA for a long time, I would find several that might interest you and your family or friends.

Then I would spend at least a weekend visiting each area to see if they have the following:

- ❖ a good quality hospital especially if you have seniors that could be living with you
- ❖ a Walmart, grocery store/s, several fast food and other restaurants
- ❖ a good educational system where your children can either attend or be allowed home schooling

- quality law enforcement, who follow the Second Amendment; fire personnel and EMTs
- an assortment of religious facilities
- several consignment stores (we have at last count over 40 here!)
- qualified health providers both allopathic and holistic
- qualified service providers for vehicle repair, appliances, electronics, computers, etc.

Of course I am sure you can add to this list. By the way here in Macon County NC we check off on this list and also add a beautiful greenway running by the Little Tennessee River; a 900 plus indoors amphitheater; gem mines; the Fun Factory for every video game imaginable, several restaurants, a laser game layout, racing cars, indoor golf game, etc.; a brand new library; Southwest Community College; a totally renovated community center; a seniors community center; art galleries, dozens of beauty salons; a 5 star café featured on the Food Channel; excellent services for military veterans; and the list goes on!

If you decide you would like to join us, my long time friend Linda, who is also a retired real estate broker and newspaper reporter, can help you. If not here, then make sure you select a qualified real estate broker that you enjoy working with! Personally I would select someone like Linda, who was in the Top 5 here in Macon County.

Make sure that ALL your family or friends (yes children and teens!) have a say in selecting the SAFE AREA! For instance, one of your members might like fishing and hunting. Here in Macon County that is covered along with Appalachian Trail hiking; canoeing; mountain climbing; mountain biking; camping; fitness with three facilities; a skate board facility; etc.

I recommend you do my Crayola Method:

Find a large enough room that you can cover in paper and have each person select a crayon color and make a name tag in his/her selected color. Now the facilitator encourages everyone to stand beside the papered wall and write out or draw his/her thoughts, ideas, desires, and suggestions for a period of 2-3 minutes.

For instance, one member might put up "stream" and "North Carolina." Another might put up "North Carolina" and "lakes." Still another might put up "lakes" and "Tennessee." At the end of the allotted time, the facilitator will then encourage every one to walk around the room and look at the other people's contributions.

The member who liked "lakes" would then circle the word "lakes" in his/her color. Each person who liked the idea of being near "lakes' would circle "lakes" at every place on the paper. This enables the group to see visually how many people are interested in "lakes" as a key elemental the SAFE AREA. This process would probably take about 5- 10 minutes. Of course, this would depend on the size of the group.

At this point the facilitator would look at the different circled words/images and select several that had the most colored circles. Let's say "lakes" was one of those words. The facilitator would encourage those people who selected "lakes" to get together and share among each other their thoughts, ideas and suggestions. This process could be repeated for other circled words.

The first discussion would continue for the allotted time of 7 minutes. Then the facilitator would blow a whistle or ring a bell. Now the members would be asked to move to another group. For instance, those in the "lakes" group would go to the "North Carolina" or "Tennessee" or "Georgia" group. Again, this group would spend 7 minutes discussing among themselves. At the whistle blow or ringing of the bell, the groups would change to the third and final group of the session.

At the end of the third session, the facilitator would recess the group for 10-15 minutes. Encourage the members to take a small pad (like Sir Richard Branson) and pen with them during the break period. During this time the facilitator and assistant would take down the old paper and re-paper the walls. Do not throw away the other paper! The facilitator ranks the circled words according to which one had the most colored circles; i.e., "lakes" had 10 of the 20 people in the group. The facilitator then ranks the circled words on one sheet in the center of the room where everyone can see the results. The entire process is now ready to be repeated a second time before lunch or evening break.

As you can see this takes TIME AND EFFORT! However this is exactly what you want as this SAFE AREA is going to be most likely a COSTLY INVESTMENT! You might live in tents for a while but eventually you are going to have to consider more permanent structures.

Okay again I can not stress enough the importance of making several weekend trips to the SAFE AREAS that you and the group are considering. I would also encourage you to NOT stay in the comfort of a hotel, motel or bed and breakfast. You need to bring your tents and stay at some property like I did with my Tent Living experience. If you selected Macon County, we would send you to the incredible Standing Indian Park, where the Appalachian Trail passes through. Then you are less than several miles from downtown Franklin, NC.

Or you might be allowed to stay on the piece of property you are looking at buying. However BEFORE you buy visit with your neighbors! From personal experience especially in western North Carolina and north Georgia, these born and bred folks are REAL suspicious of outsiders!

Let me give you several incidents that happen to my friends that were considered "outsiders".

My business associate Ron moved to Rabun County Georgia from Atlanta. He bought a place on beautiful Lake Rabun. When he would go into nearby Clayton he would pass a house, where an old timer would be sitting on the porch. Ron would always wave at the old timer, but the old timer and life long resident of Rabun County would IGNORE the friendly wave!

Ron said this went on for TEN YEARS! Then one day at almost exactly TEN YEARS the old timer WAVED at Ron!

Another more serious experience happened to my friend and wealthy multi-millionaire Tom, who came to Tellico Plains, Tennessee with the plans to renovate this little village into a tourist destination. Well Tom made the BAD mistake of not checking to see if the life time residents and powers-to-be wanted his vision. Evidently they did not because after Tom purchased several homes in the area they mysteriously BURNED TO THE GROUND!

Tom finally got the message. He sold his multi-million dollar home and moved away! To this day Tellico Plains has NO motel and the downtown area has turned into a ghost town! If these people had participated in Tom's vision there would be more EMPLOYMENT for these NARROW-MINDED folks!

So make sure you are at least welcomed in your chosen SAFE AREA. It helps greatly if you have a real estate expert like Linda, who knows almost everybody in town!

You also want to make sure that one of you learns about the geography and soil in your potential selections. For instance, I'm sure that several of your members might want to grow their own vegetables and even learn to can them. Your real estate broker/agent SHOULD know the right people to direct you to. Here are some more suggestions:

The US Geological Survey Water Sources Division can usually answer your questions about hydrology, water as a resource and hydrological mapping and can be reached at 800-462-9000 or at their web site. They also have many other resources through their Earth Science Information Centers located throughout the United States.

If you are looking for a well drilling company you will want to contact the National Ground Water Association.

Another valuable resource is the US Department of Agriculture with their aerial maps. Also the Farm Service Agency in each US County can be very helpful. The US Forestry Service offers information on soil studies in areas near U.S. forests.

Each state has offices of Cooperative State Extension Service and you will find out more about the areas you are considering. The National Conservation Resource Center works with local soil and water conservation districts.

Also don't forget *The Old Farmer's Almanac* just because your grandparents relied on it and you think that it has gone out of style! Far from it. The Almanac, which has been published since 1792, has very reliable information about planting, nation-wide weather forecasts, best days for fishing, correction tables for the tides, consumer trends, trivia, etc. You will want to have a printed copy of the latest Almanac as well as get ones from the past as they have articles that are timeless!

Other resources for you to consider: local board of health, local building inspector, local universities and colleges, state mineral agencies and the Research Center Directory at your local library.

Well that should keep you and your group busy for awhile!

As I mentioned before, you and the group will have to consider PERMANENT shelter either presently or in the near future. Up here it gets REAL cold in December and around the middle of that month during my Tent Living experience it hit 17 DEGREES! That was just too cold for my 68 year young body at the time. So I found that my friend Linda had her deceased father's apartment for reasonable rent. I moved right in and as I write this I'm nice and warm in its cozy quarters!

I have ALWAYS had a fascination with DOMES ever since I spent several years studying with Marshall Thurber, who was the right-hand man to the world famous Buckminster (Bucky) Fuller, futurist and creator of the geodesic dome.

Years later I found Robert Lassiter, a builder of The DODECAHEDRON DOME, which is much stronger than Bucky's dome. In fact, it is the STRONGEST man-made structure on Planet Earth. So I arranged to go to Greenville, NC to learn to build this dome you see in the VIDEO (https://youtu.be/gk6QVC0cJkY). By the way ignore about how to reach us as you see in the video. Also the quality sucks as it was made well over 10 years ago with a tiny "dinosaur" handheld cam! You can contact me at mrvalentineknightstemplar@gmail.com Subject: Dome.

I most recently have also become fascinated with the TINY HOME MOVEMENT and we are pleased to announce that we now are associated with the creator of both of the 160 square foot homes you see here. The container home you might have seen on HGTV.

Our latest venture we are calling our XP Eco LLC (http://www.xpecollc.com) Eco-Village, which you see a rendering of here that was specifically done for Sir Richard Branson's Team working to restore the British Virgin Islands. Sir Richard sees for both his Necker Island and the entire British Virgin Islands a future vision of GREEN AND SUSTAINABLE. We offer both with the Crank-A-Watt ™, the dodecahedron dome, the tiny container home, the Bioponica bio-secure food system, Global SunOven, Survivor Industries products, solar panels and wind generating systems connected to versions of the Crank-A-Watt ™, etc.

Ironically at XP Eco LLC we were making plans to move our business to Saint Croix, US Virgin Islands when the two devastating hurricanes slammed into the area. That has been put on indefinite hold. Also

STUPIDLY the USVI government would not let their own people buy from us! Go figure!

So now we have told Virgin Unite and the BVI government we would entertain the idea of moving our business there and training their people how to build our XP Eco LLC Eco-Village for their islands and other areas of the Caribbean. As I write this book, the Virgin Unite Team has contacted me saying they will be soon looking at not just recovery but the implementation of Sir Richard's vision like we have presented and you see here.

In early 2018 we will be selling this entire ECO-VILLAGE ONLINE! We will manufacture and supply EVERYTHING you see from our US operation in Franklin, North Carolina. Just email me at mrvalentineknightstemplar@gmail.com Subject: Eco-Village Dealerships

And if this version does not float your boat then may be the one rendered below that we will be building in western North Carolina in Macon County in 2018 will do the trick!

Okay we have come to the end of this manual; however, many of you will be beginning your EXCITING LIFE-SAVING journey and I will assure you that it will have NO end! I have been involved since 1999 and I'm still learning so much!

As promised here is a PROMISE I wrote on my whiteboard: "I PROMISE on or before 3/4/2021 XtremePreparedness LLC will be a BILLION dollar company." Signed MR Valentine 10/12/2017.

You probably think this is a ridiculous promise but I truly believe that with our Team Preparedness and suppliers currently and those to come we will do it! Not for my personal EGO but because currently there is NO DOMINATING company in the Situational Awareness, Preparedness and Survival niche! WHY NOT US!

If you would like to be put on my emailing list or have any questions and most importantly suggestions, please email me at mrvalentineknightstemplar@gmail.com and Subject: XtremePreparedness

MR Valentine

Ephesians 6:13

NOTES:

BONUS!

It is the second oldest profession in the world. No, it is not prostitution – that's the first! Actually it is BARTER. I have bartered for thousands of dollars worth of products and services including a Mercedes and a Cadillac and even a house I lived in costing only utilities. It was a nice old 1920s bungalow with hardwood floors and three fireplaces on 1.5 acres.

You should first do an audit of the number of potential skills you can offer through barter. I did that audit and to my surprise found that I have 44 different skills I could offer through barter! For instance, I was able to barter staying in a 1896 inn for over two years because I offered the owners my skills in marketing, public relations and helping to run the inn based on my previous experience of running a nightclub/restaurant. When the inn experienced a devastating fire that required extensive renovation, I learned how to strip floors, paint like a pro, develop a professional inventory for the insurance company and polyurethane the floors. This two year experience actually would qualify me to run an inn on my own if I so desired. (Been there done that, NEXT!)

After you have taken your audit, take time to find what might be the top three that people would pay the most to learn from you or use your skills. With over 19 years in Internet/Web 2 Marketing, I am able to offer people a complete up-to-date web based marketing plan including setting up Social Media pages on Facebook, Twitter, LinkedIn, etc. Furthermore with over 30 years in Video/TV production, I can teach people how to shoot and edit simple videos to promote their business or cause.

Every time you barter, do not do it so that you can acquire frivolous items like clothes, trips and even dinners. Barter with people who have items that you can turn into assets like the classic Mercedes I still wish I had. When I bartered for the mint condition 1973 Mercedes I did it for $2500 in barter for my public relations skills for a kitchen designer. Today the Mercedes would be worth up to $40,000! Other assets would be art, jewelry, antiques, collectibles, **WEAPONS, AMMO** and definitely cool 60s or earlier cars!

The best barter deal you can do is where you barter for an asset and then flip it for CASH! Here is how you do that. Let's use the Mercedes for example. I could have kept the Mercedes garaged instead of driving it. I could have run an inexpensive ad in the original *Robb Report*. I most likely would have found a buyer of the Mercedes right in the Atlanta area for $5000-$7500. I had $2500 in barter in it, and the ad might have cost another $100 in cash. So let's say that I had $2600 out laid in barter and cash. My cash net could have been $2400- $4900!

Today with the Social Media and eBay, it is easier than in the early 1980s. For instance, I have a friend that owned one of the premiere Southwest Native American collectible stores in the world. I could have gone to Jay and offered to develop a Social Media campaign for the store and bartered for one of the nice pieces of silver jewelry, artwork, pottery or baskets. I would know what the comparable piece was going for on eBay and offer a lower price by 20%. By the way I did just that for a beautiful handcrafted gold Apache ring!

With barter, you are only limited by your imagination!

You might say the thousands of dollars of FREE Preparedness stuff I got was a form of barter. I agreed to put them on my blog posts, do a video on YouTube, and mention them in my books.

NOTES: